A QUICK & EASY GUIDE TO
THEY/THEM
PRONOUNS

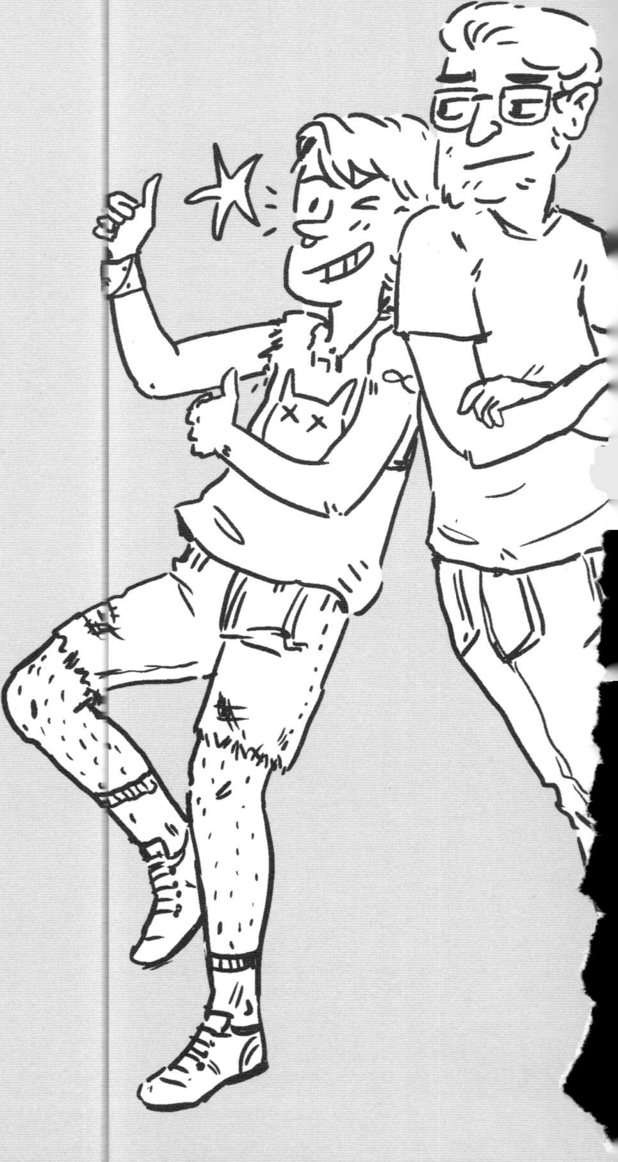

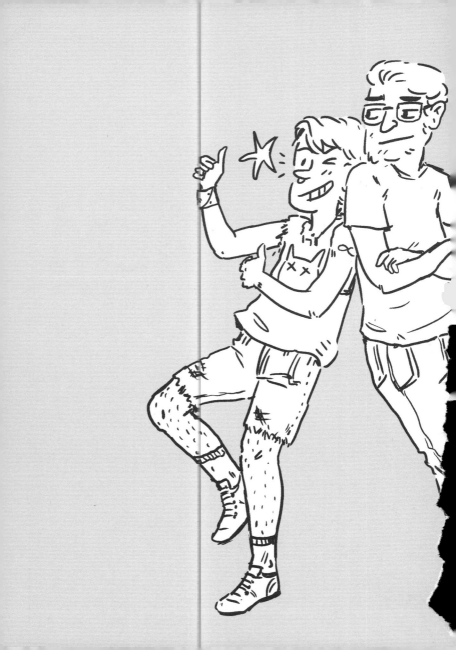

A QUICK & EASY GUIDE TO
THEY/THEM PRONOUNS

ARCHIE BONGIOVANNI & TRISTAN JIMERSON

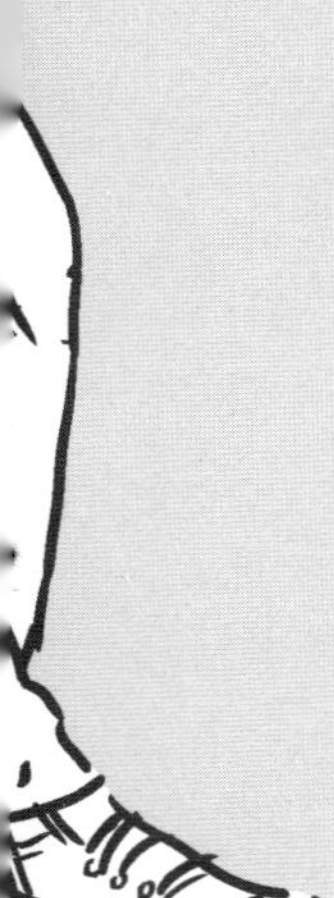

A LIMERENCE PRESS
PUBLICATION

Lettered by **CRANK!** (he/him)
Designed by **KATE Z. STONE** (she/her)
Edited by **ARI YARWOOD** (she/her)

✦ PUBLISHED BY LIMERENCE PRESS ✦

LIMERENCE PRESS IS AN IMPRINT OF ONI PRESS, INC.

JOE NOZEMACK (he/him) **founder & chief financial officer**
JAMES LUCAS JONES (he/him) **publisher**
CHARLIE CHU (he/him) **v.p. of creative & business development**
BRAD ROOKS (he/him) **director of operations**
MELISSA MESZAROS (she/her) **director of publicity**
MARGOT WOOD (she/her) **director of sales**
RACHEL REED (she/her) **marketing manager**
TROY LOOK (he/him) **director of design & production**
HILARY THOMPSON (she/her) **senior graphic designer**
KATE Z. STONE (she/her) **junior graphic designer**
SONJA SYNAK (she/her) **junior graphic designer**
ANGIE KNOWLES (she/her) **digital prepress lead**
ARI YARWOOD (she/her) **executive editor**
ROBIN HERRERA (she/her) **senior editor**
DESIREE WILSON (she/her) **associate editor**
ALISSA SALLAH (she/her) **administrative assistant**
JUNG LEE (he/him) **logistics associate**

LimerencePress.com
twitter.com/limerencepress
Limerencepress.tumblr.com

First Edition: June 2018
ISBN 978-1-62010-499-6
eISBN 978-1-62010-500-9

Library of Congress Control Number: 2017959095

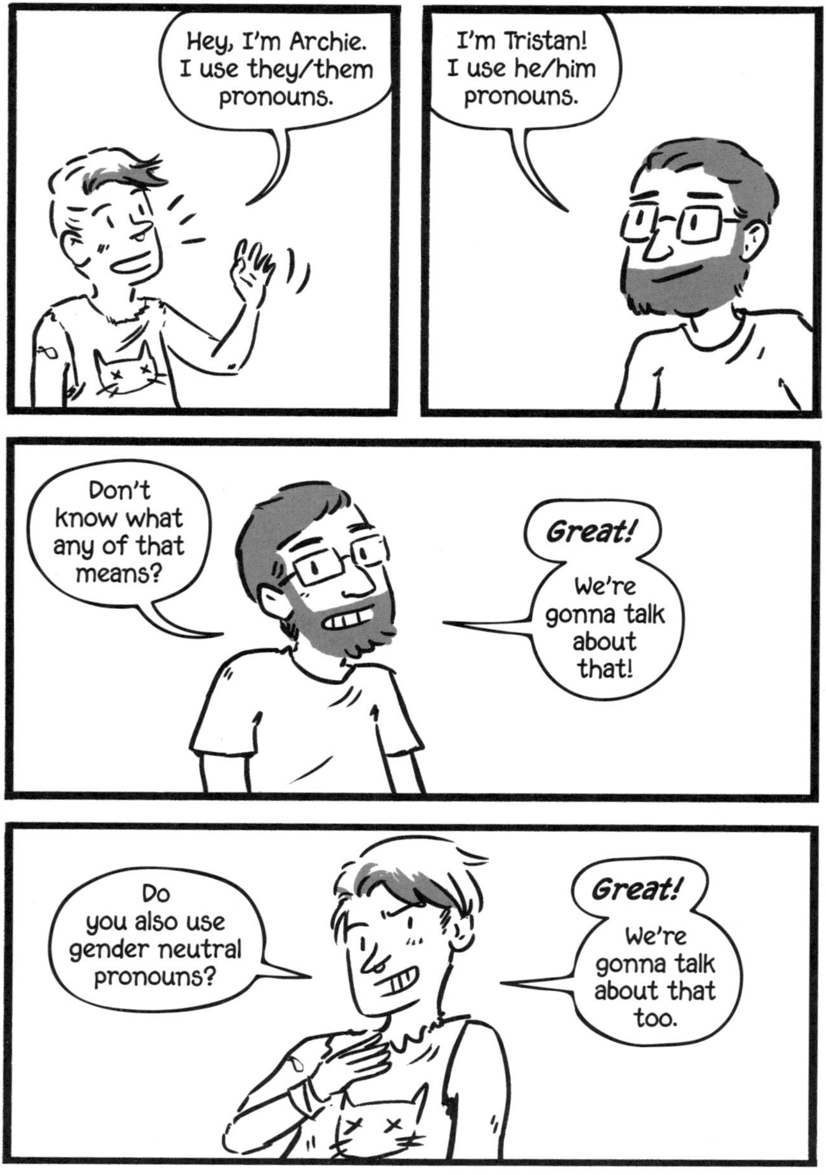
Hey, I'm Archie. I use they/them pronouns.
I'm Tristan! I use he/him pronouns.
Don't know what any of that means?
Great!
We're gonna talk about that!
Do you also use gender neutral pronouns?
Great!
We're gonna talk about that too.

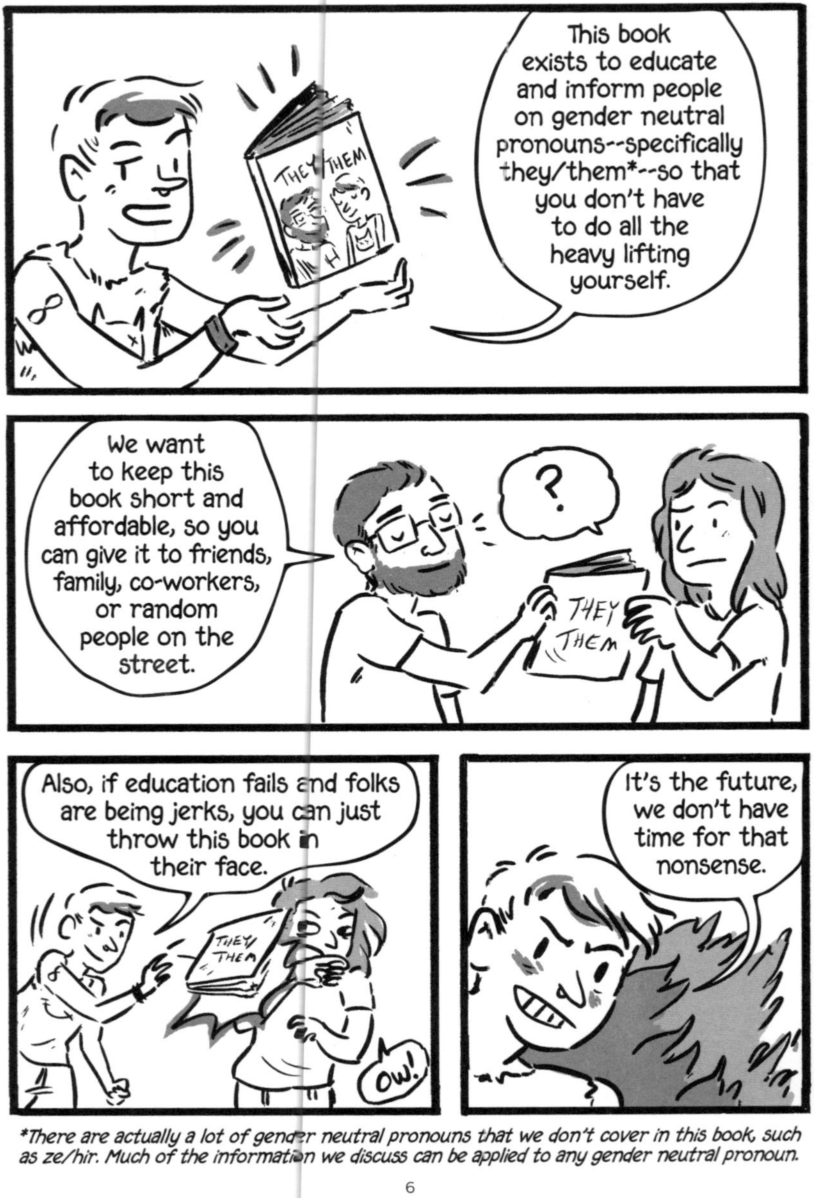
This book exists to educate and inform people on gender neutral pronouns--specifically they/them*--so that you don't have to do all the heavy lifting yourself.
THEY/THEM
We want to keep this book short and affordable, so you can give it to friends, family, co-workers, or random people on the street.
?
THEY THEM
Also, if education fails and folks are being jerks, you can just throw this book in their face.
THEY/ THEM
OW!
It's the future, we don't have time for that nonsense.

There are actually a lot of gender neutral pronouns that we don't cover in this book, such as ze/hir. Much of the information we discuss can be applied to any gender neutral pronoun.

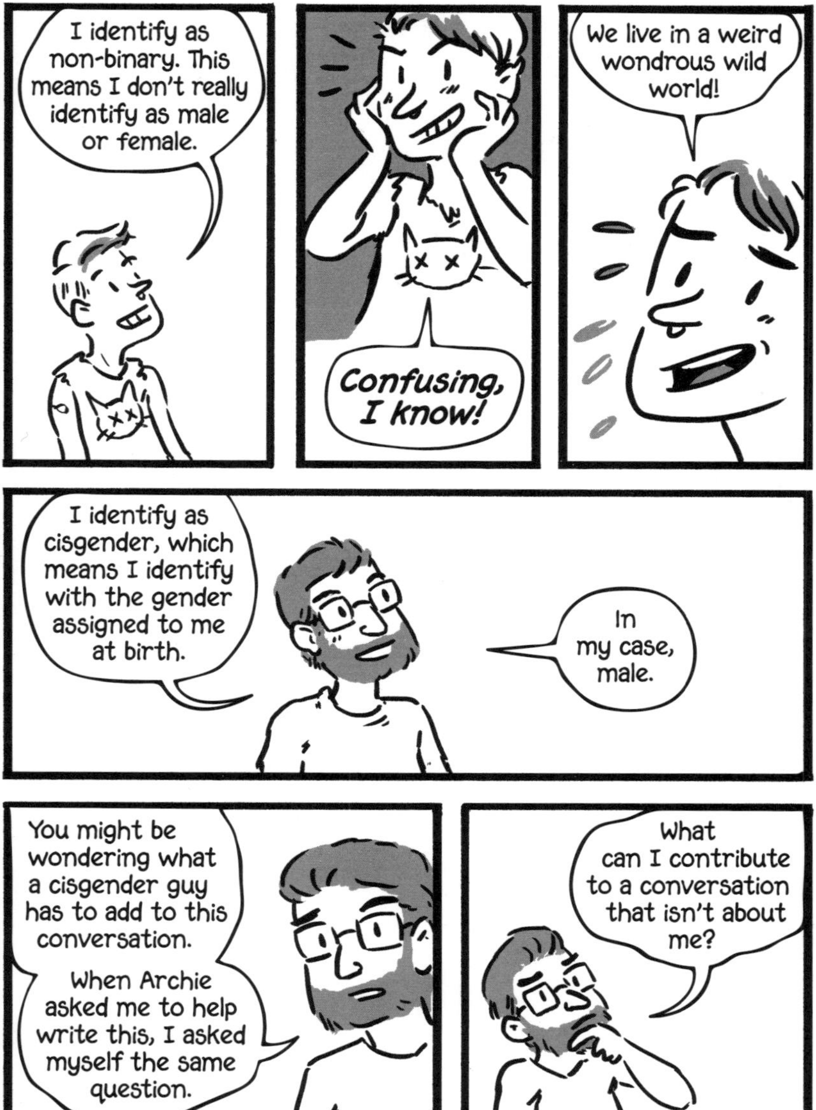
I identify as non-binary. This means I don't really identify as male or female.
Confusing, I know!
We live in a weird wondrous wild world!
I identify as cisgender, which means I identify with the gender assigned to me at birth.
In my case, male.
You might be wondering what a cisgender guy has to add to this conversation.
When Archie asked me to help write this, I asked myself the same question.
What can I contribute to a conversation that isn't about me?

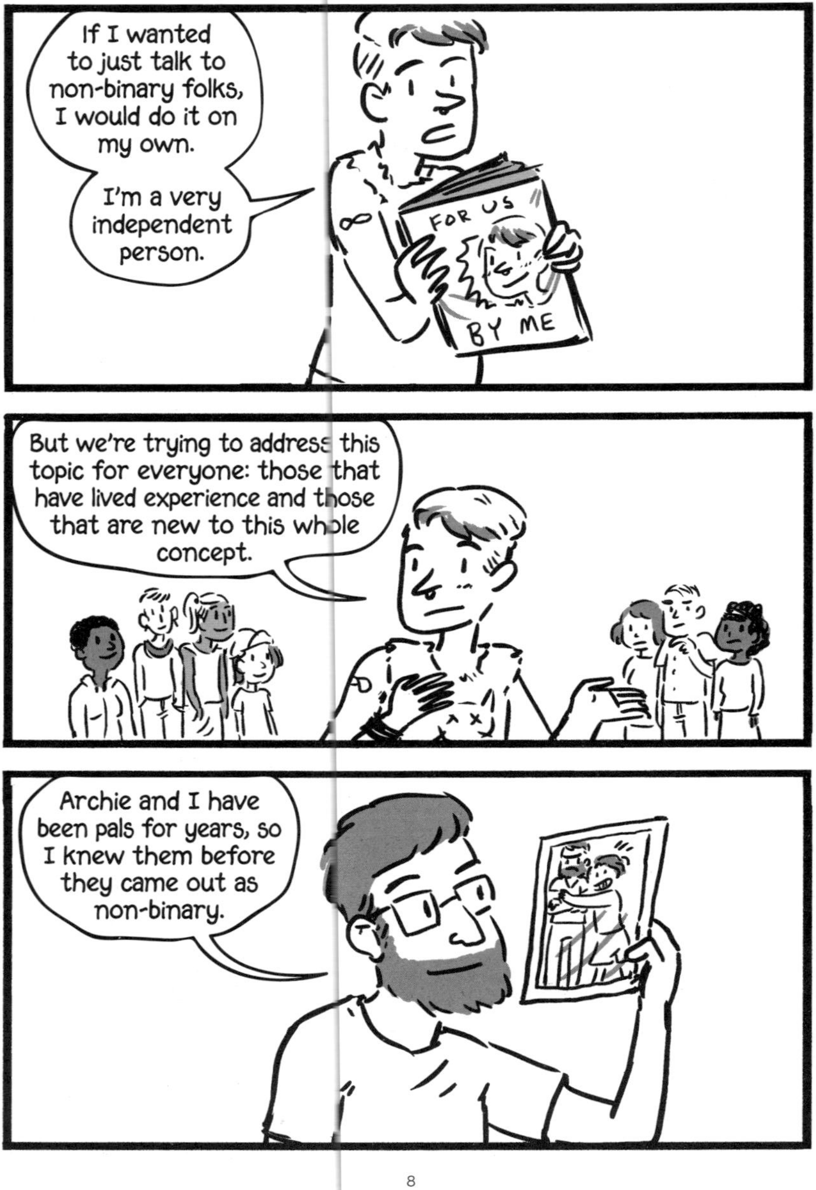
If I wanted to just talk to non-binary folks, I would do it on my own.
I'm a very independent person.
FOR US
BY ME
But we're trying to address this topic for everyone: those that have lived experience and those that are new to this whole concept.
Archie and I have been pals for years, so I knew them before they came out as non-binary.

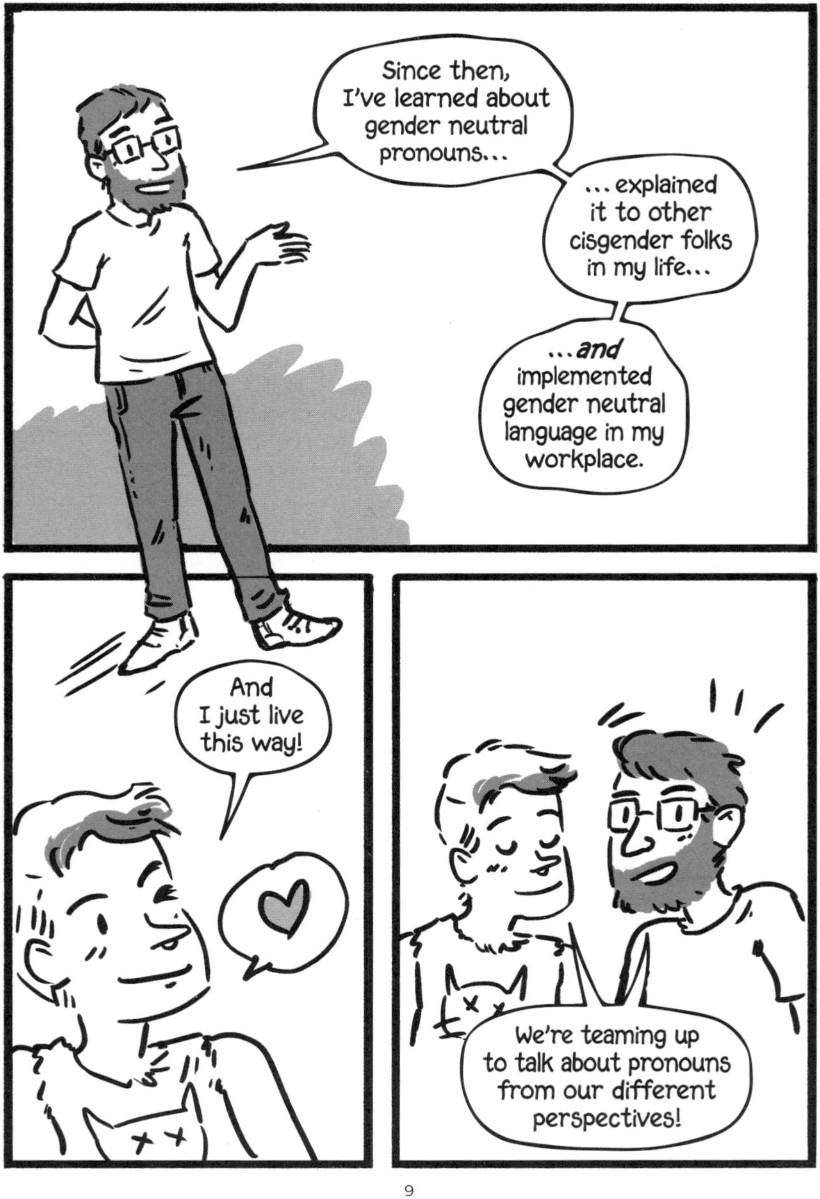
Since then, I've learned about gender neutral pronouns...
...explained it to other cisgender folks in my life...
...*and* implemented gender neutral language in my workplace.
And I just live this way!
We're teaming up to talk about pronouns from our different perspectives!

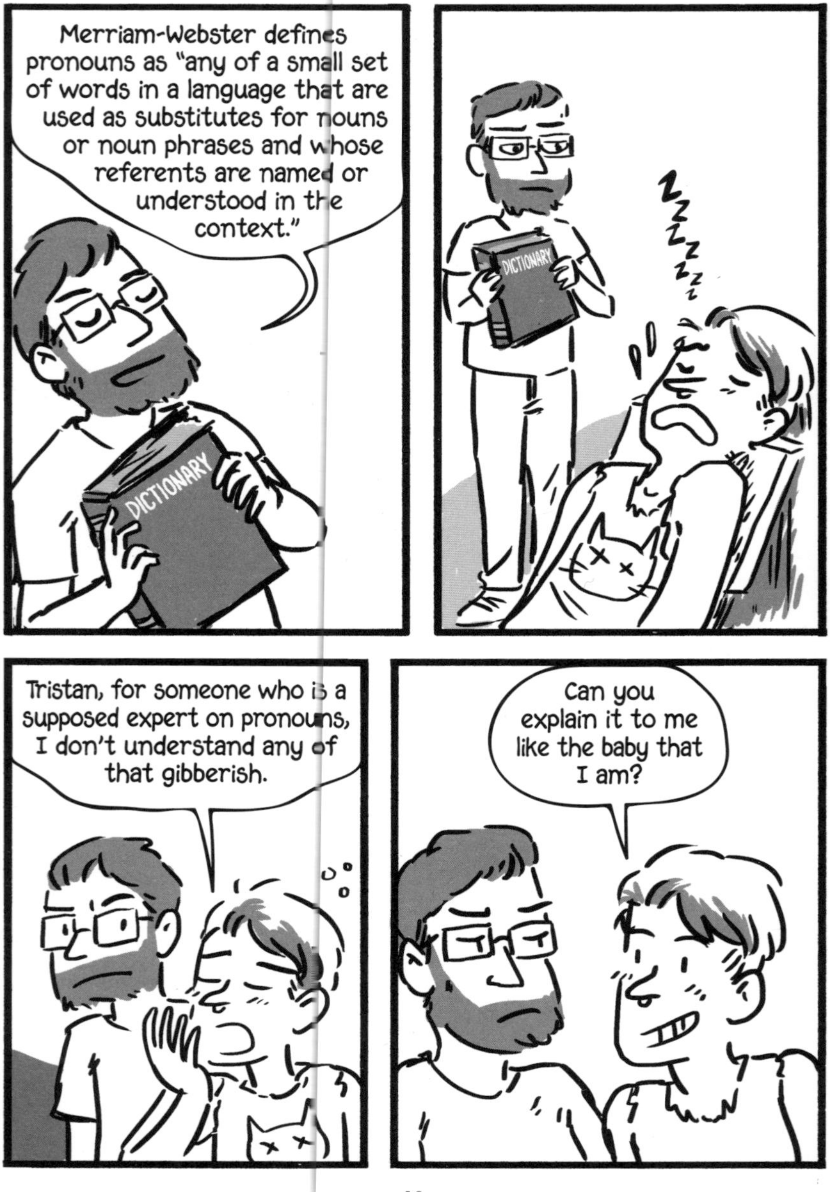
Merriam-Webster defines pronouns as "any of a small set of words in a language that are used as substitutes for nouns or noun phrases and whose referents are named or understood in the context."
DICTIONARY
DICTIONARY
ZZZZZZZ
Tristan, for someone who is a supposed expert on pronouns, I don't understand any of that gibberish.
Can you explain it to me like the baby that I am?

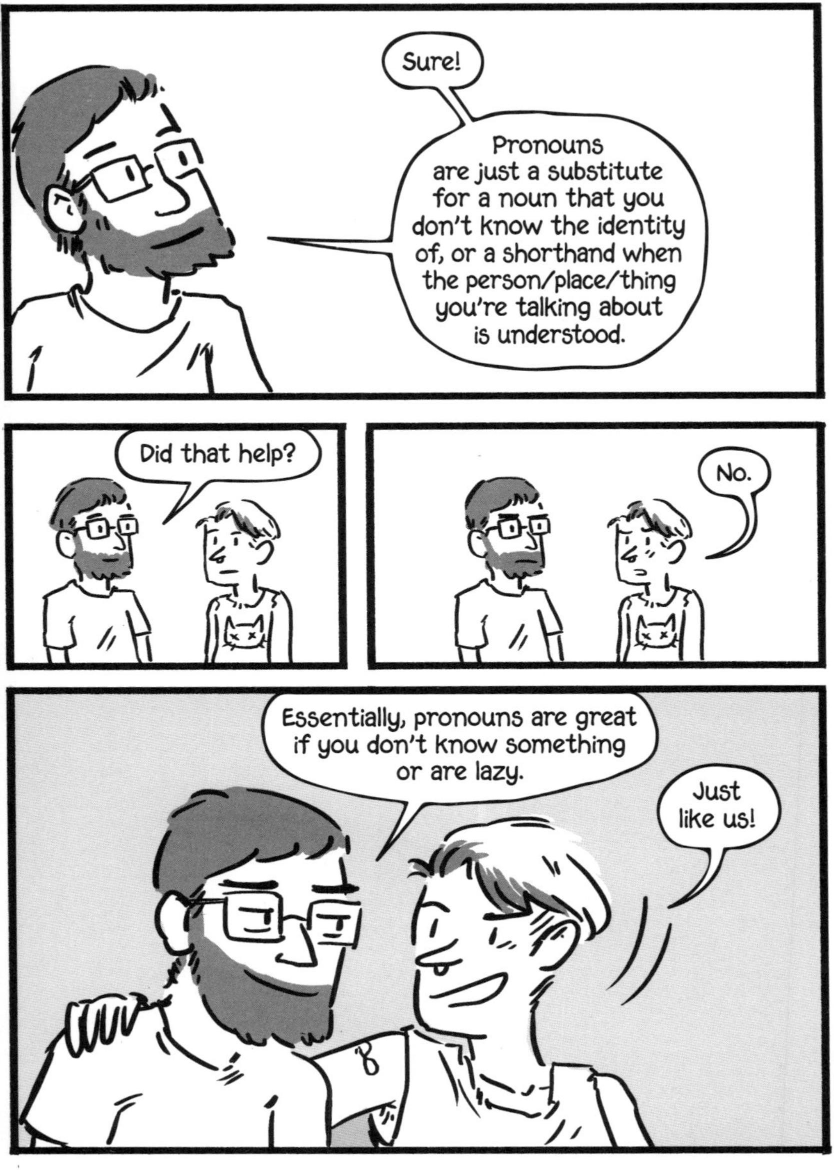
Sure!
Pronouns are just a substitute for a noun that you don't know the identity of, or a shorthand when the person/place/thing you're talking about is understood.
Did that help?
No.
Essentially, pronouns are great if you don't know something or are lazy.
Just like us!

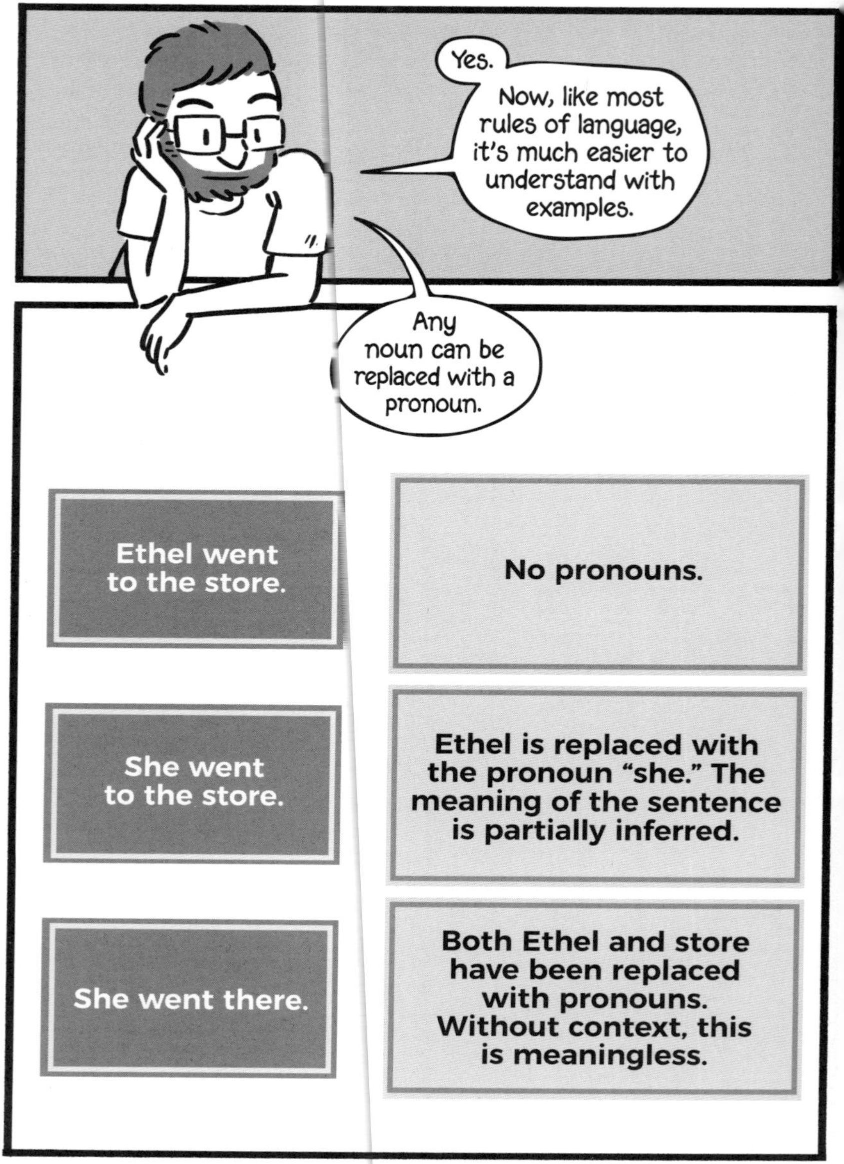
Yes.
Now, like most rules of language, it's much easier to understand with examples.
Any noun can be replaced with a pronoun.
Ethel went to the store.
No pronouns.
She went to the store.
Ethel is replaced with the pronoun "she." The meaning of the sentence is partially inferred.
She went there.
Both Ethel and store have been replaced with pronouns. Without context, this is meaningless.

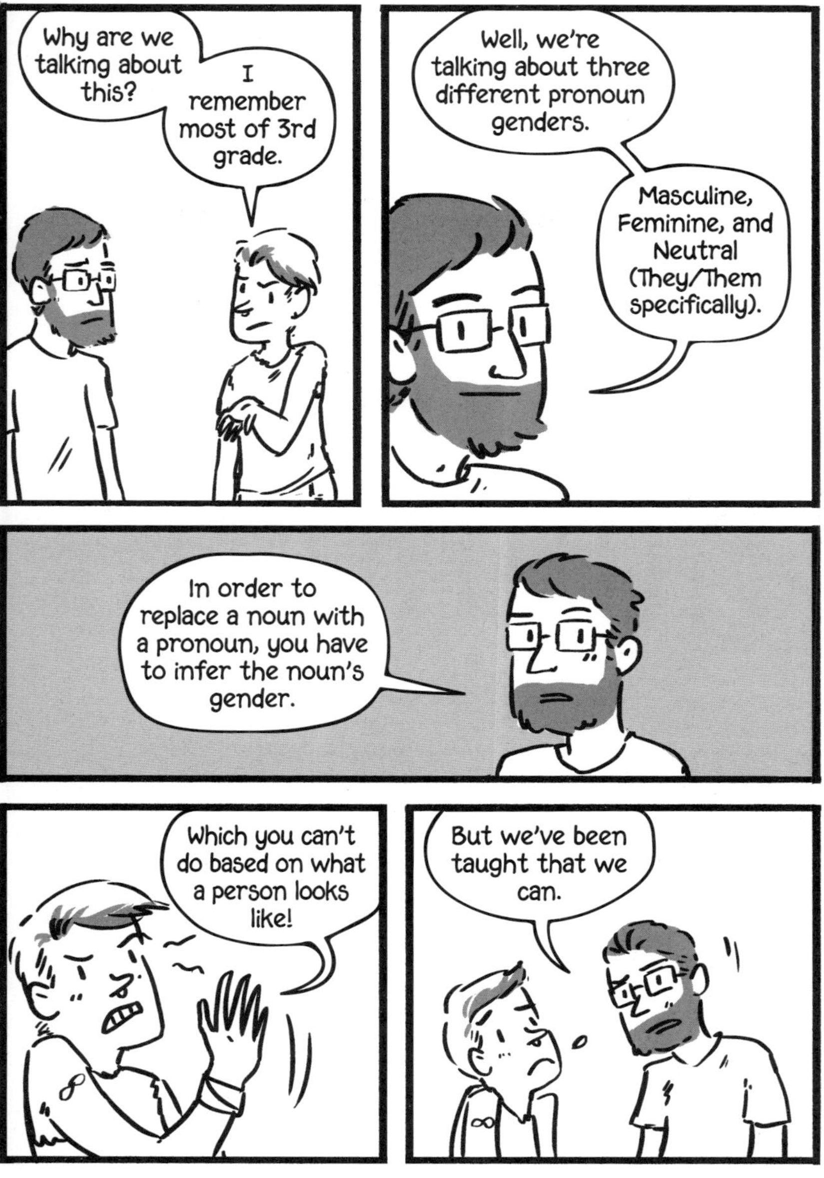
Why are we talking about this?
I remember most of 3rd grade.
Well, we're talking about three different pronoun genders.
Masculine, Feminine, and Neutral (They/Them specifically).
In order to replace a noun with a pronoun, you have to infer the noun's gender.
Which you can't do based on what a person looks like!
But we've been taught that we can.

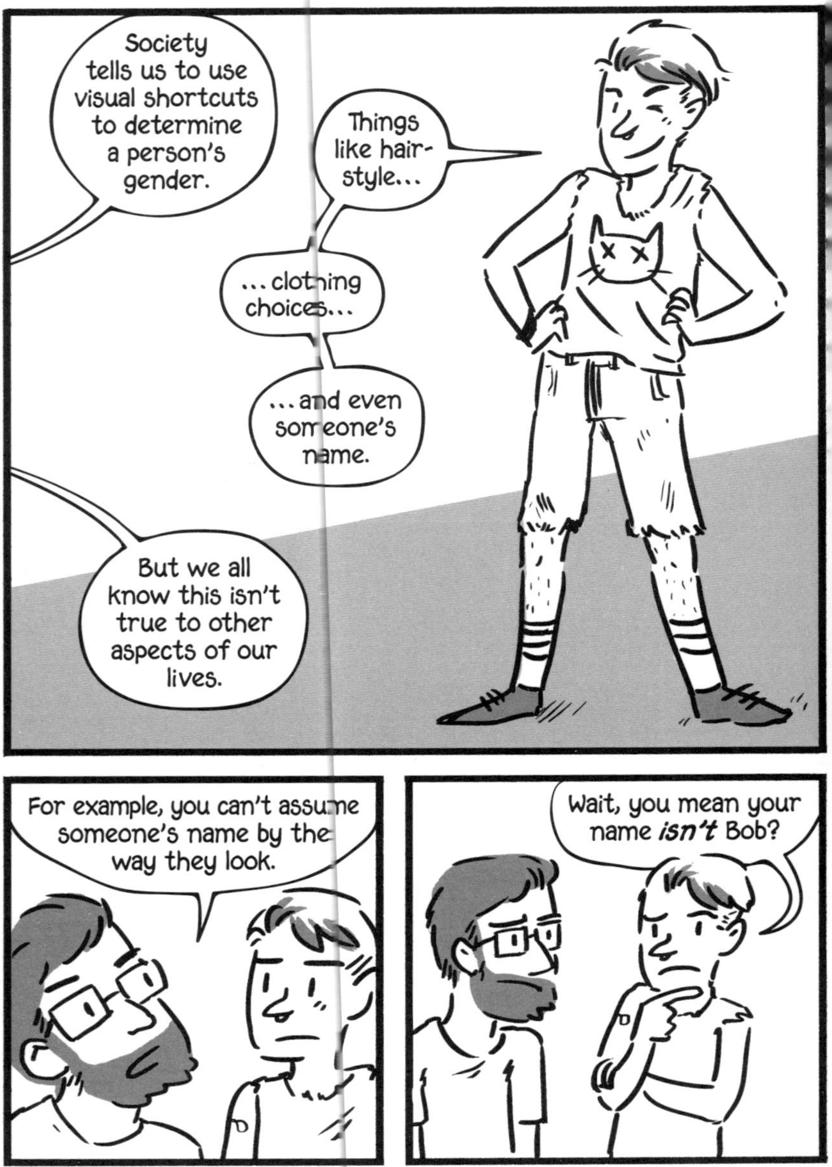
Society tells us to use visual shortcuts to determine a person's gender.
Things like hair-style...
...clothing choices...
...and even someone's name.
But we all know this isn't true to other aspects of our lives.
For example, you can't assume someone's name by the way they look.
Wait, you mean your name *isn't* Bob?

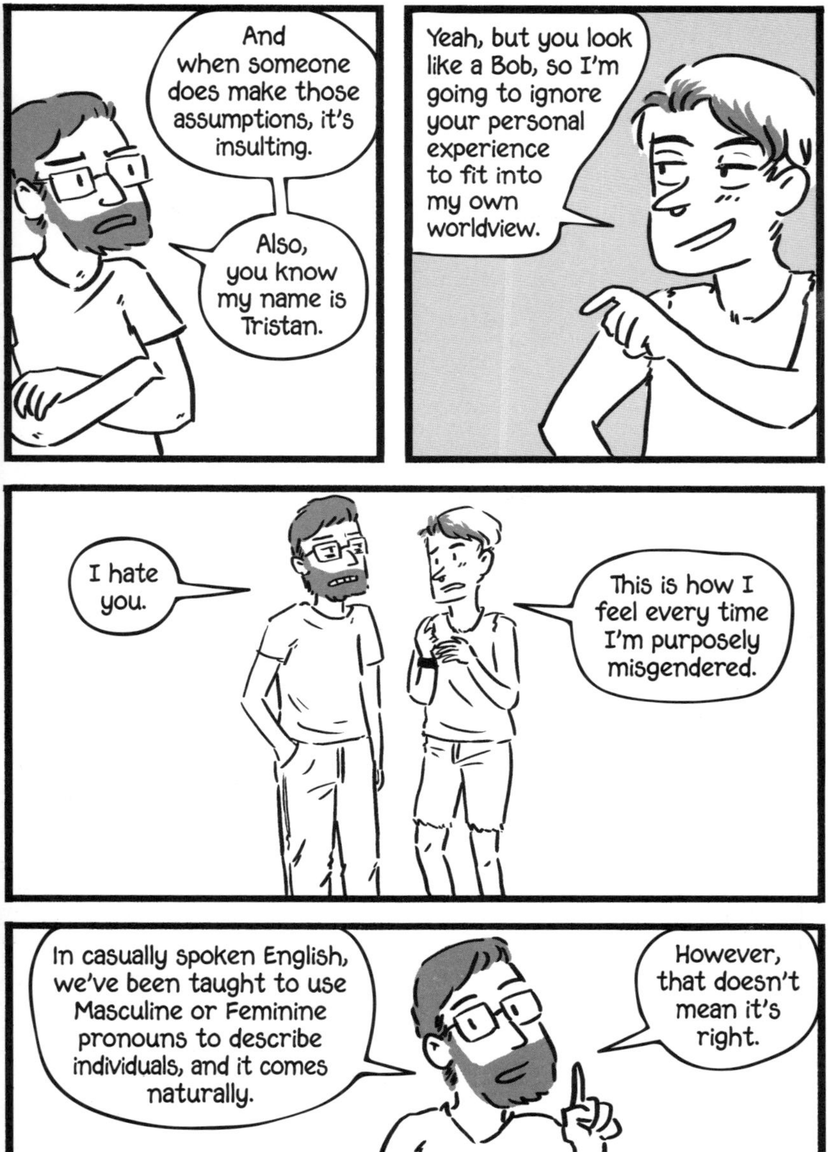

And when someone does make those assumptions, it's insulting.
Also, you know my name is Tristan.
Yeah, but you look like a Bob, so I'm going to ignore your personal experience to fit into my own worldview.
I hate you.
This is how I feel every time I'm purposely misgendered.
In casually spoken English, we've been taught to use Masculine or Feminine pronouns to describe individuals, and it comes naturally.
However, that doesn't mean it's right.

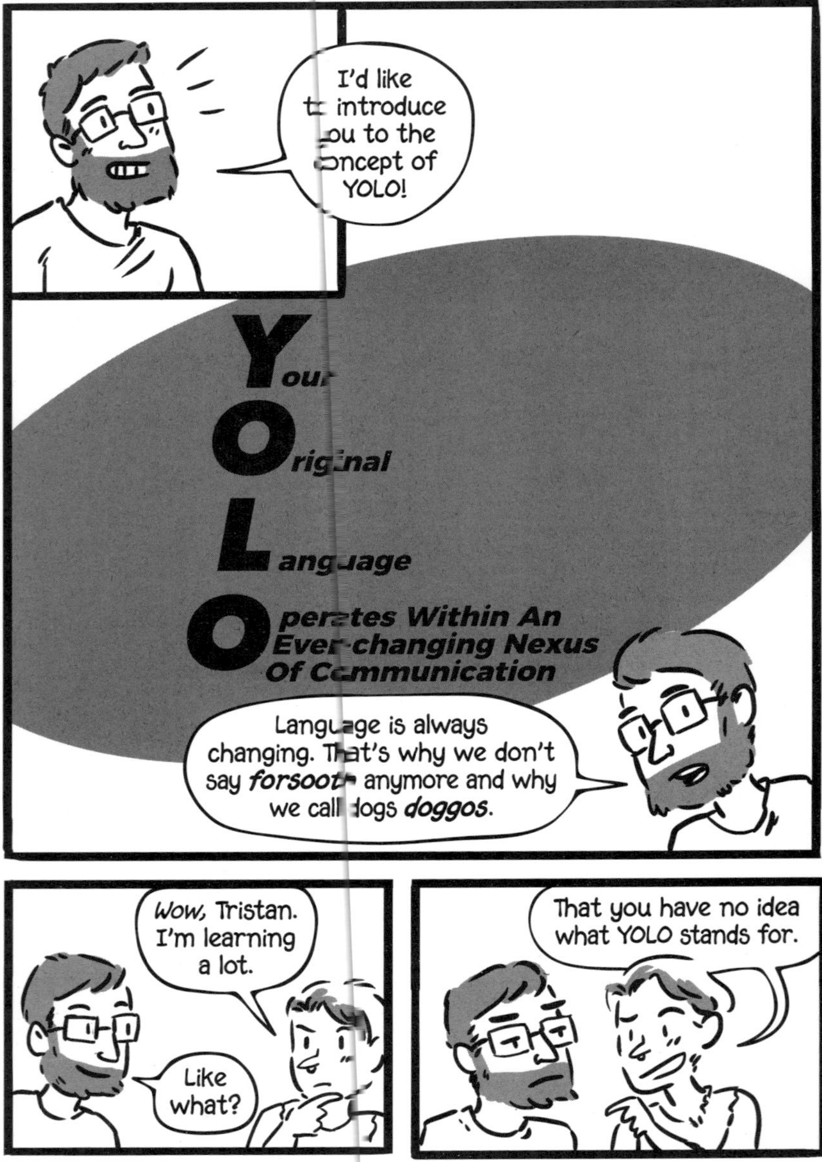
I'd like to introduce you to the concept of YOLO!
Your
Original
Language
Operates Within An Ever-changing Nexus Of Communication
Language is always changing. That's why we don't say *forsooth* anymore and why we call dogs *doggos*.
Wow, Tristan. I'm learning a lot.
Like what?
That you have no idea what YOLO stands for.

A QUICK REFERENCE CHART FOR YOUR CONVENIENCE!

Subject	Object	Possessive determiner	Possessive pronoun	Reflexive
She	Her	Her	Hers	Herself
He	Him	His	His	Himself
They	Them	Their	Theirs	Themself
Ze	Hir	Hir	Hirs	Hirself
Carol	Carol	Carol's	Carol's	Carol

Here's what it all looks like next to each other! I included one of the (many) gender neutral pronouns besides they/them (in this case ze/hir).

Also, some folks don't want any pronouns associated with themselves and prefer for us to just use their names.

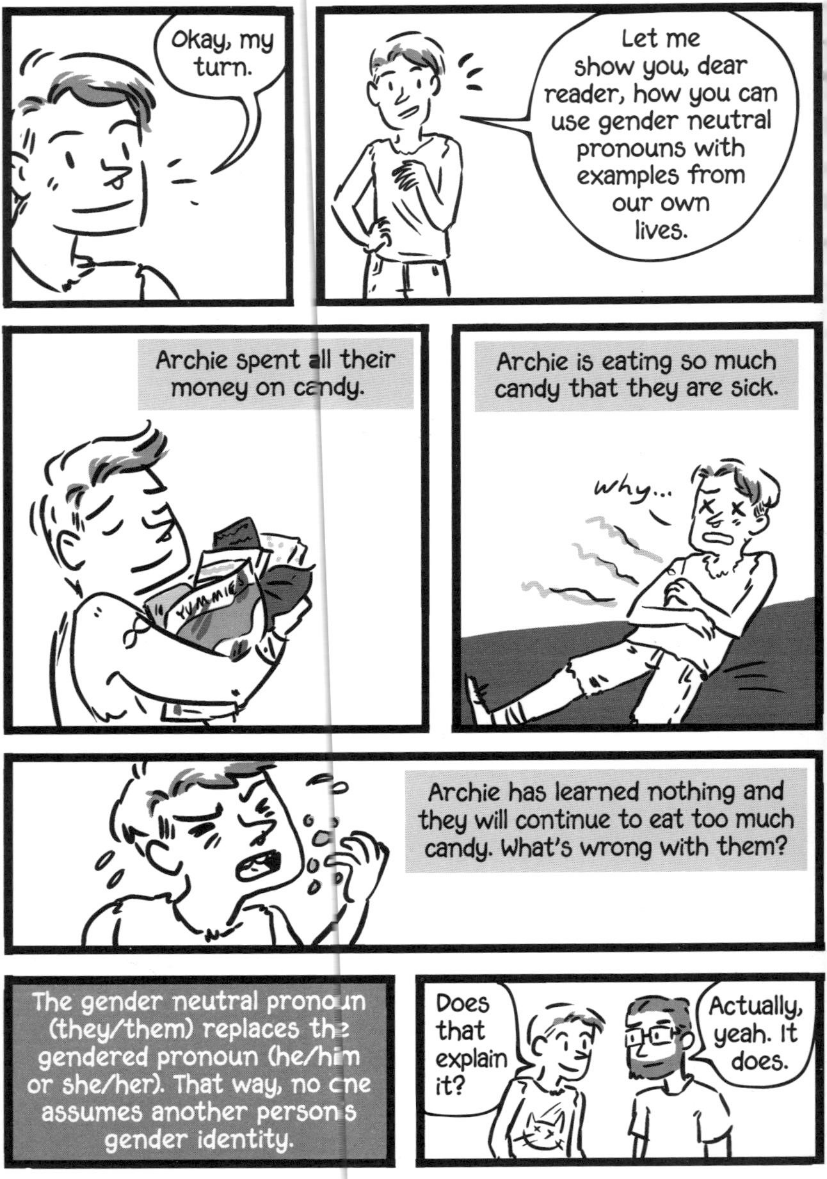

Okay, my turn.
Let me show you, dear reader, how you can use gender neutral pronouns with examples from our own lives.
Archie spent all their money on candy.
Archie is eating so much candy that they are sick.
why...
YUMMIES
Archie has learned nothing and they will continue to eat too much candy. What's wrong with them?
The gender neutral pronoun (they/them) replaces the gendered pronoun (he/him or she/her). That way, no one assumes another person's gender identity.
Does that explain it?
Actually, yeah. It does.

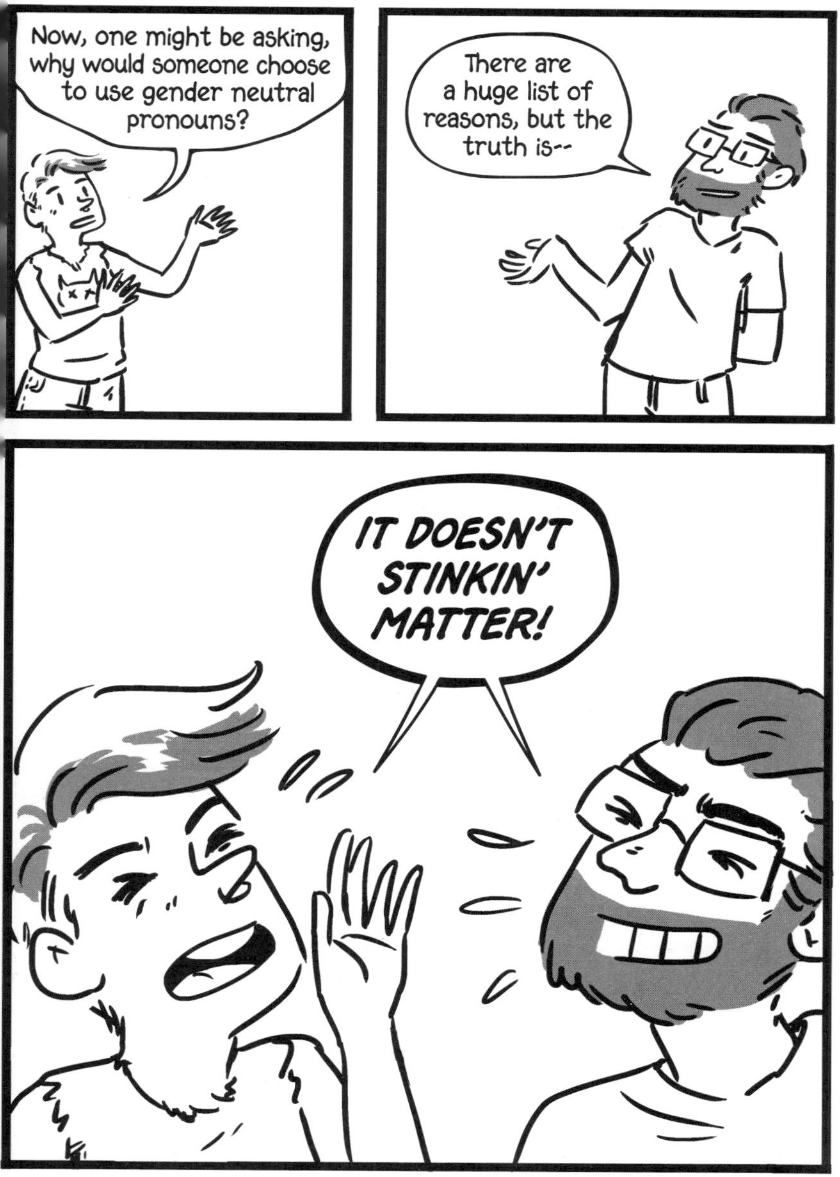
Now, one might be asking, why would someone choose to use gender neutral pronouns?
There are a huge list of reasons, but the truth is--
IT DOESN'T STINKIN' MATTER!

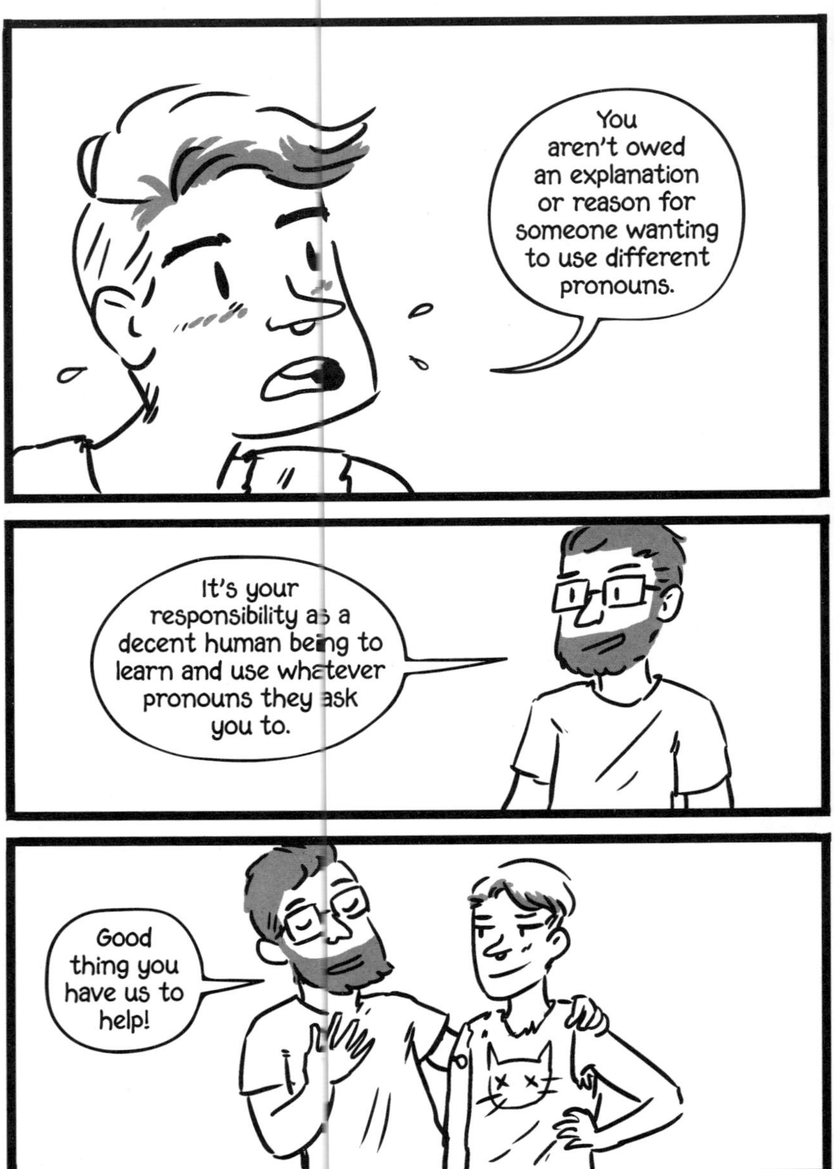
You aren't owed an explanation or reason for someone wanting to use different pronouns.
It's your responsibility as a decent human being to learn and use whatever pronouns they ask you to.
Good thing you have us to help!

WHY PRONOUNS MATTER

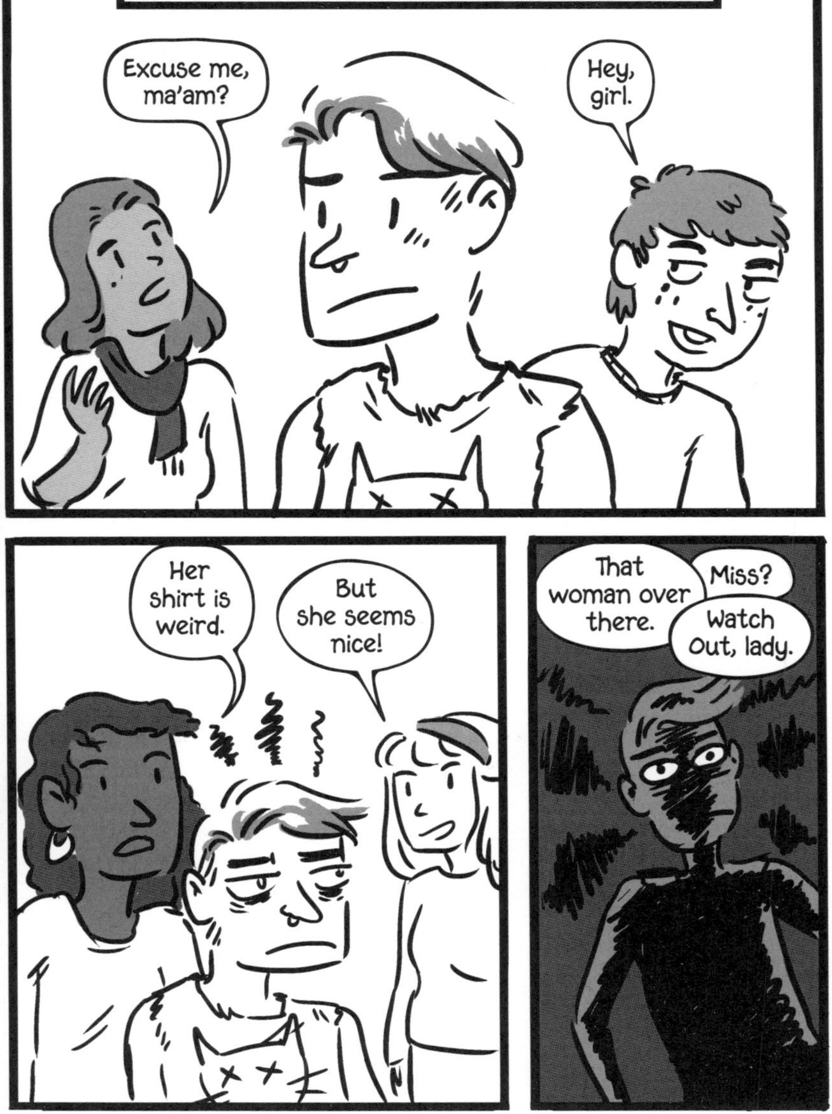
Excuse me, ma'am?
Hey, girl.
Her shirt is weird.
But she seems nice!
That woman over there.
Miss?
Watch out, lady.

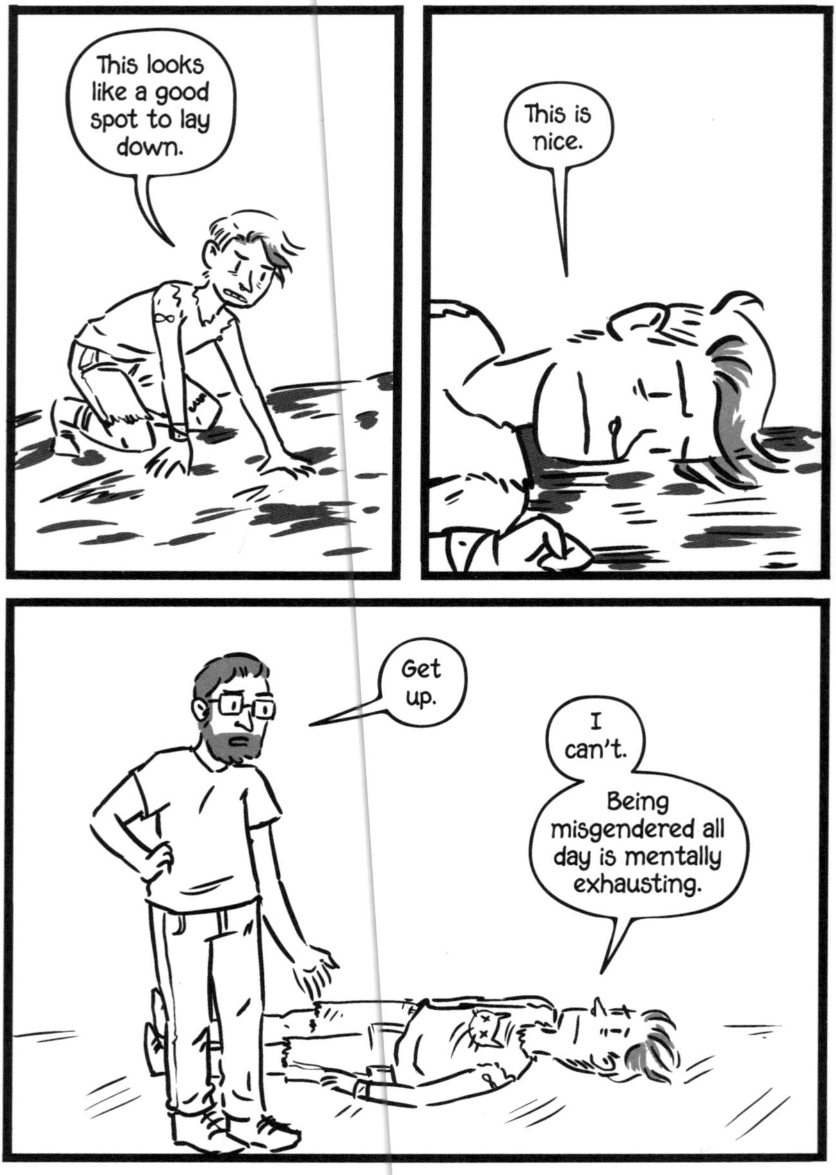
This looks like a good spot to lay down.
This is nice.
Get up.
I can't.
Being misgendered all day is mentally exhausting.

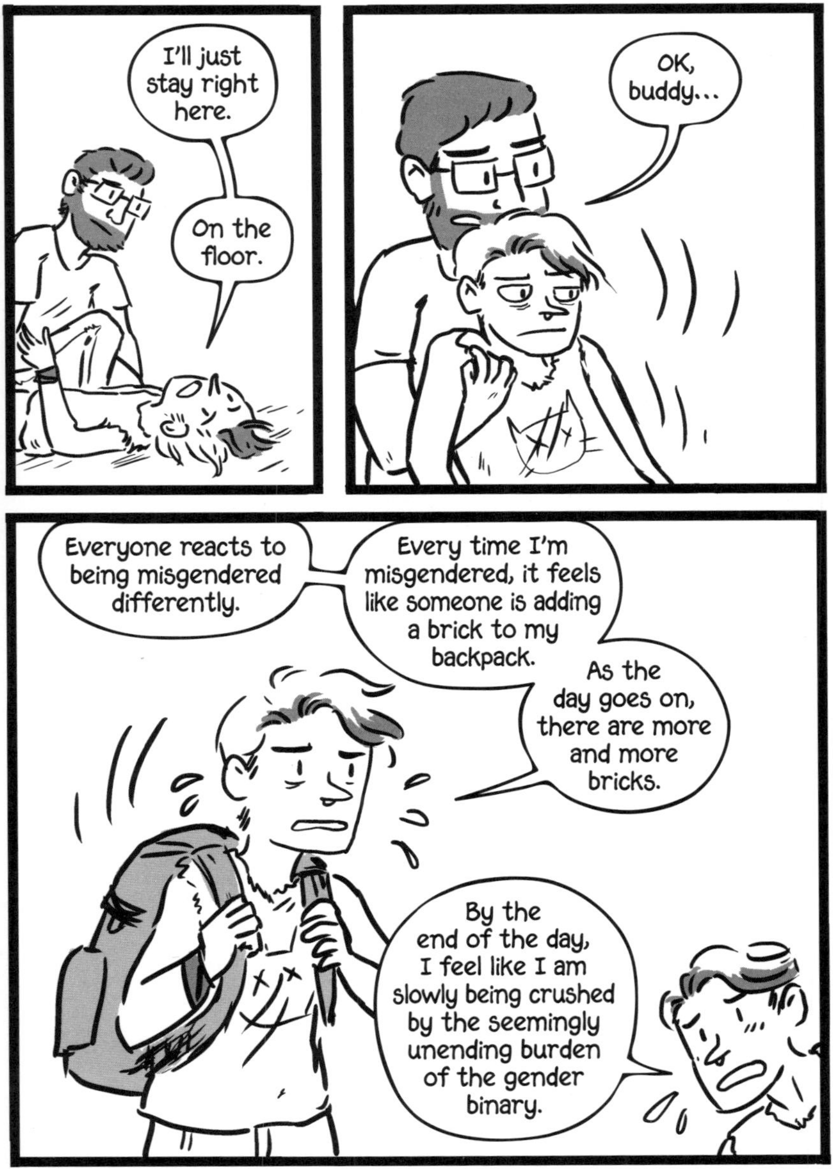
I'll just stay right here.
On the floor.
OK, buddy...
Everyone reacts to being misgendered differently.
Every time I'm misgendered, it feels like someone is adding a brick to my backpack.
As the day goes on, there are more and more bricks.
By the end of the day, I feel like I am slowly being crushed by the seemingly unending burden of the gender binary.

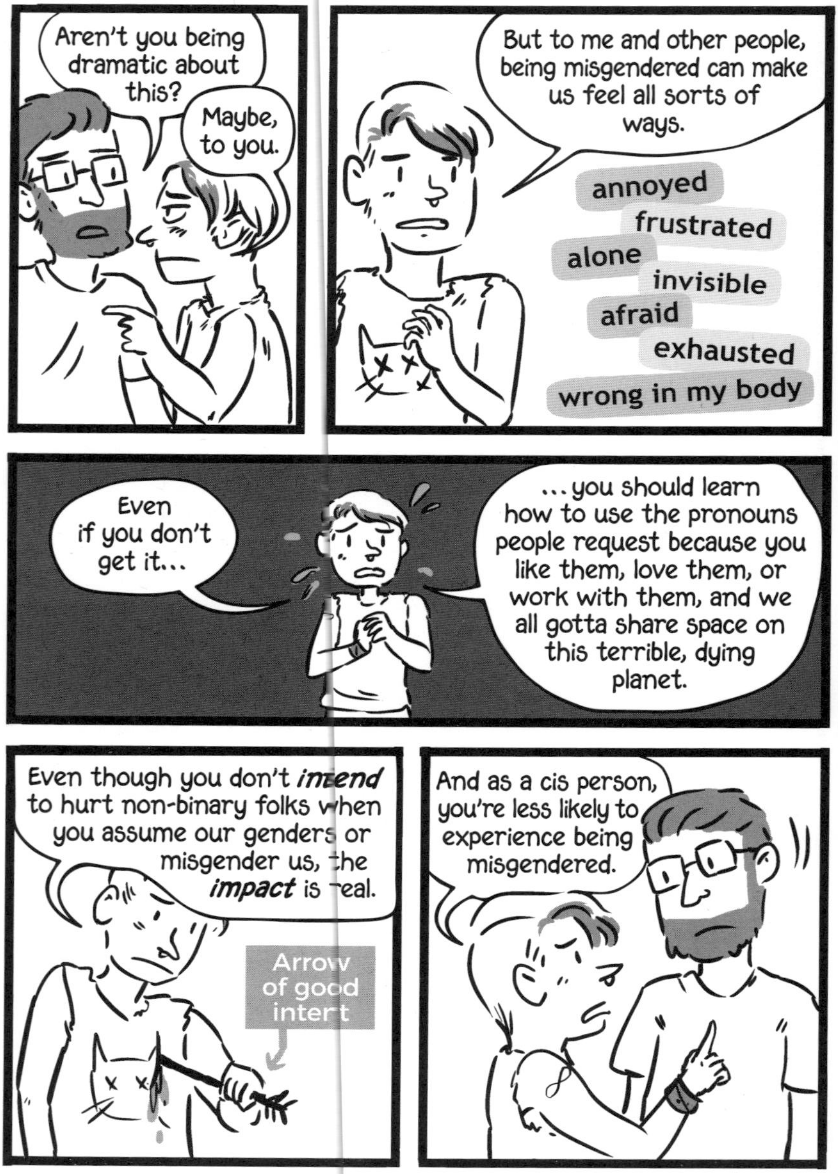
Aren't you being dramatic about this?
Maybe, to you.
But to me and other people, being misgendered can make us feel all sorts of ways.
annoyed
frustrated
alone
invisible
afraid
exhausted
wrong in my body
Even if you don't get it...
...you should learn how to use the pronouns people request because you like them, love them, or work with them, and we all gotta share space on this terrible, dying planet.
Even though you don't *intend* to hurt non-binary folks when you assume our genders or misgender us, the *impact* is real.
Arrow of good intent
And as a cis person, you're less likely to experience being misgendered.

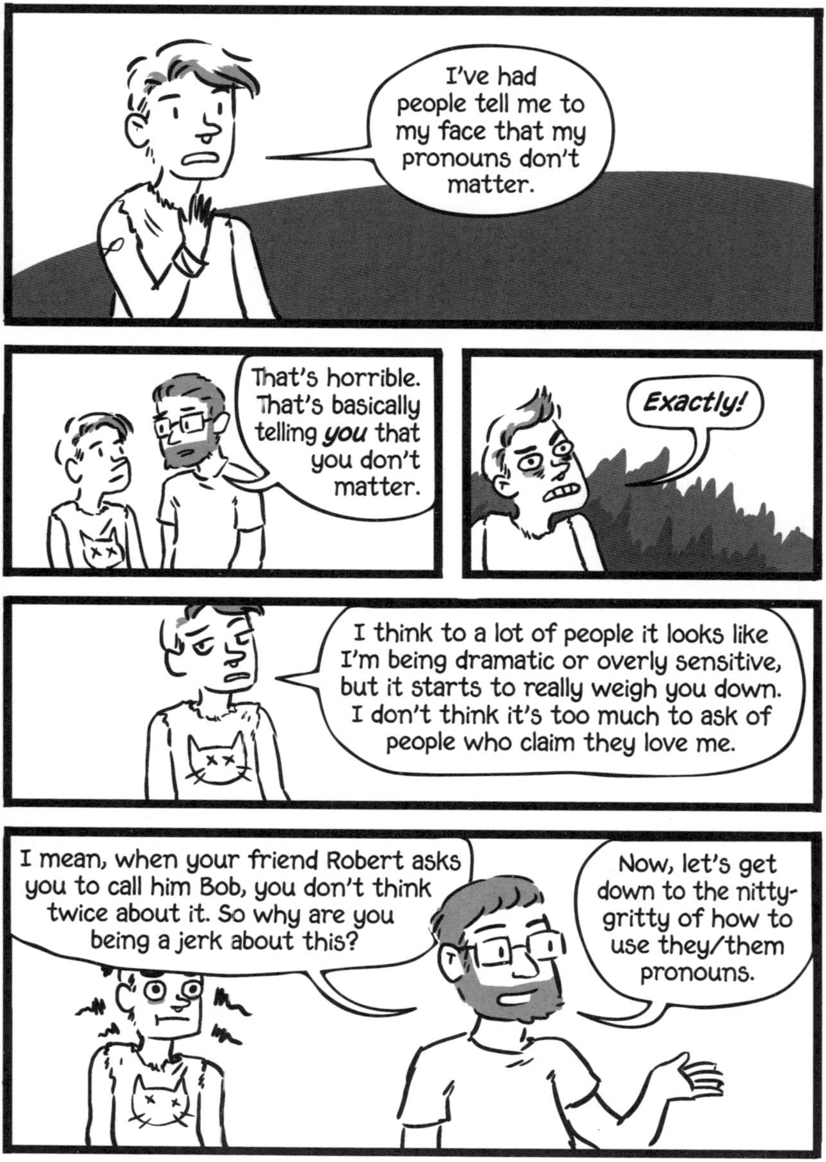

I've had people tell me to my face that my pronouns don't matter.
That's horrible. That's basically telling *you* that you don't matter.
Exactly!
I think to a lot of people it looks like I'm being dramatic or overly sensitive, but it starts to really weigh you down. I don't think it's too much to ask of people who claim they love me.
I mean, when your friend Robert asks you to call him Bob, you don't think twice about it. So why are you being a jerk about this?
Now, let's get down to the nitty-gritty of how to use they/them pronouns.

How to use They/Them pronouns in everyday life: **A practical guide!**

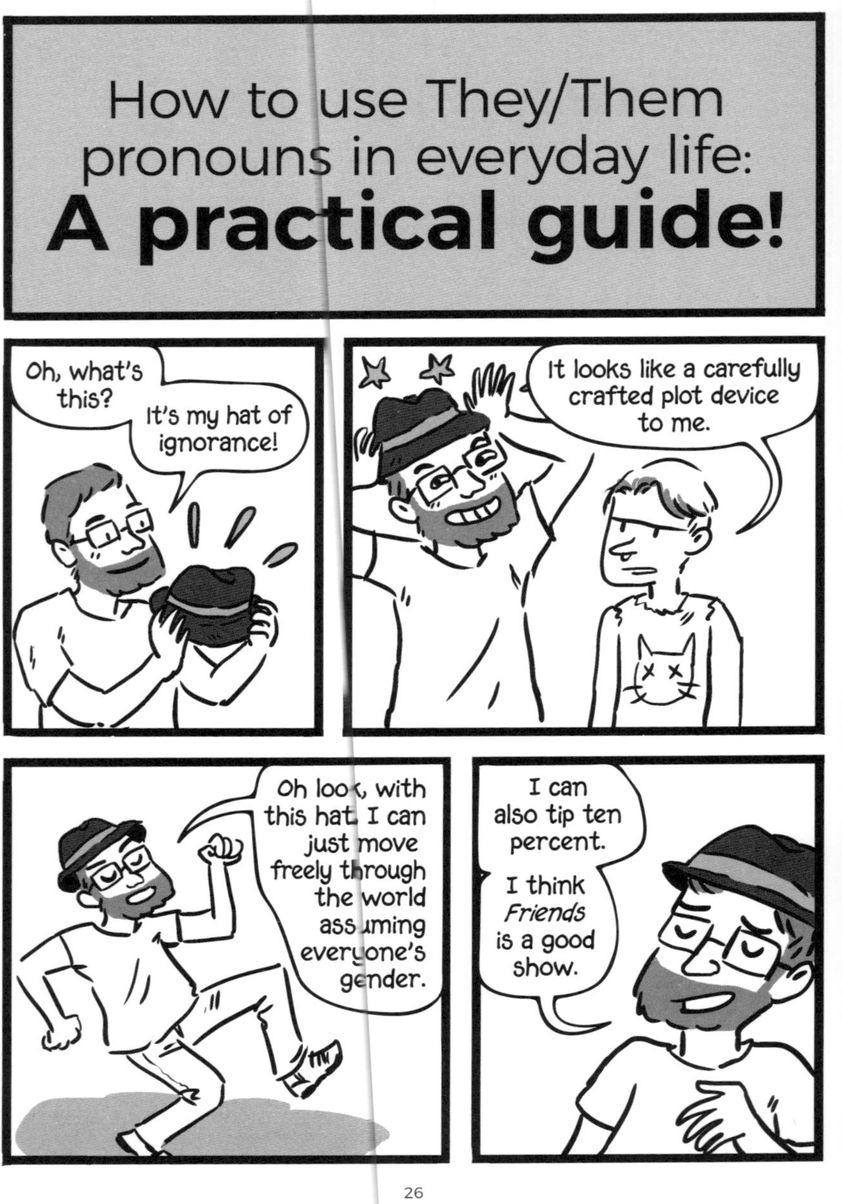
Oh, what's this?
It's my hat of ignorance!
It looks like a carefully crafted plot device to me.
Oh look, with this hat I can just move freely through the world assuming everyone's gender.
I can also tip ten percent.
I think *Friends* is a good show.

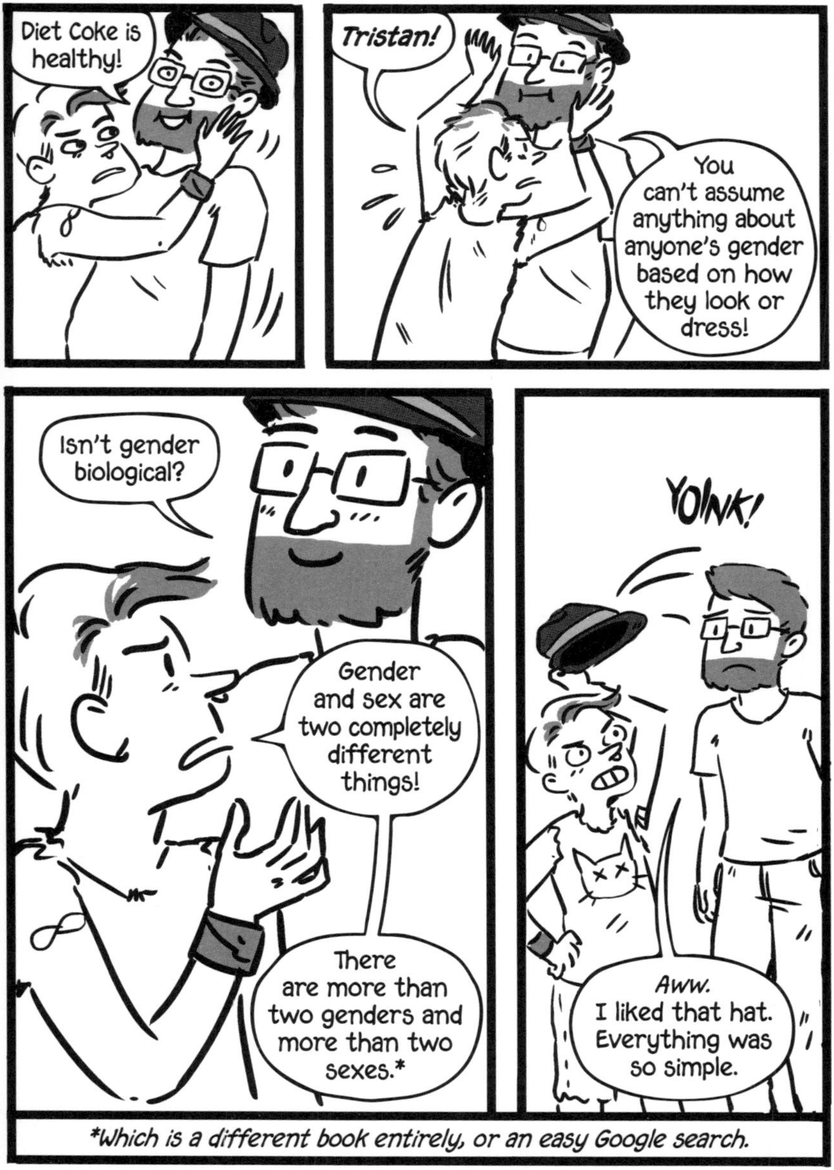
Diet Coke is healthy!
Tristan!
You can't assume anything about anyone's gender based on how they look or dress!
Isn't gender biological?
Gender and sex are two completely different things!
There are more than two genders and more than two sexes.*
YOINK!
Aww. I liked that hat. Everything was so simple.
*Which is a different book entirely, or an easy Google search.

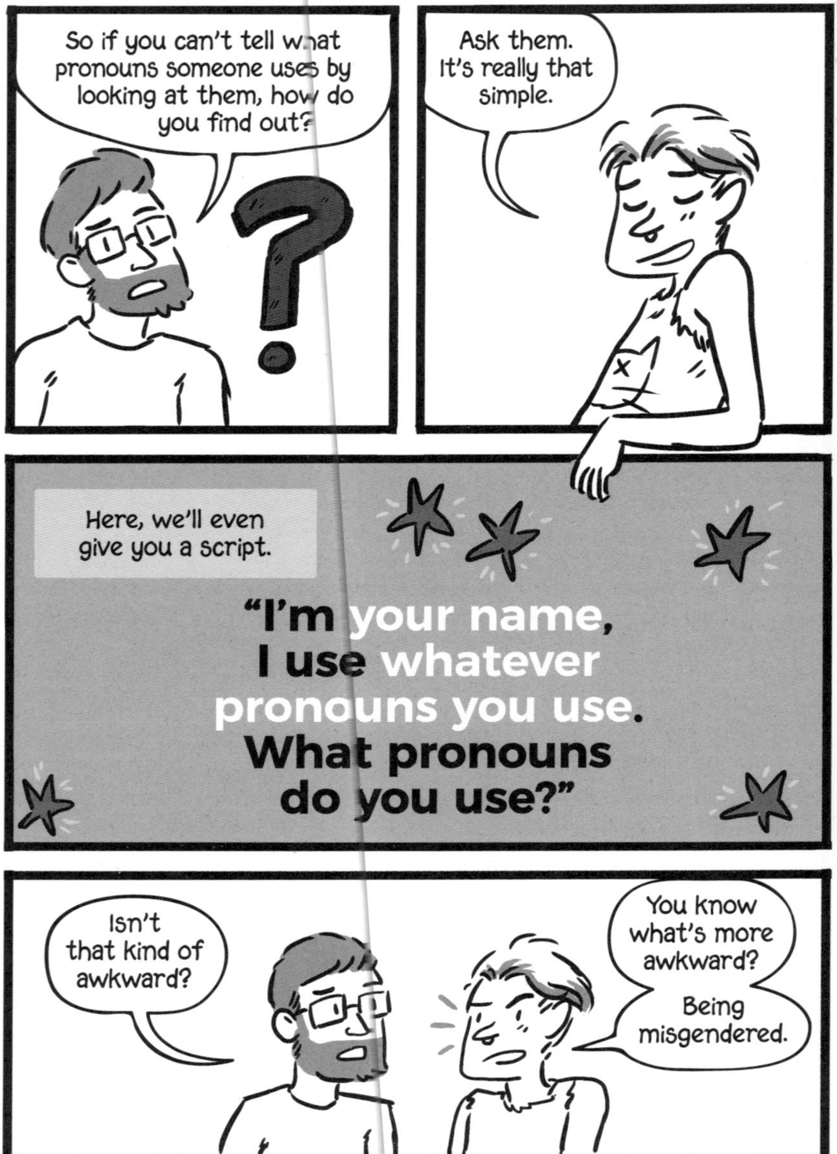
So if you can't tell what pronouns someone uses by looking at them, how do you find out?
Ask them. It's really that simple.
Here, we'll even give you a script.
"I'm your name, I use whatever pronouns you use. What pronouns do you use?"
Isn't that kind of awkward?
You know what's more awkward?
Being misgendered.

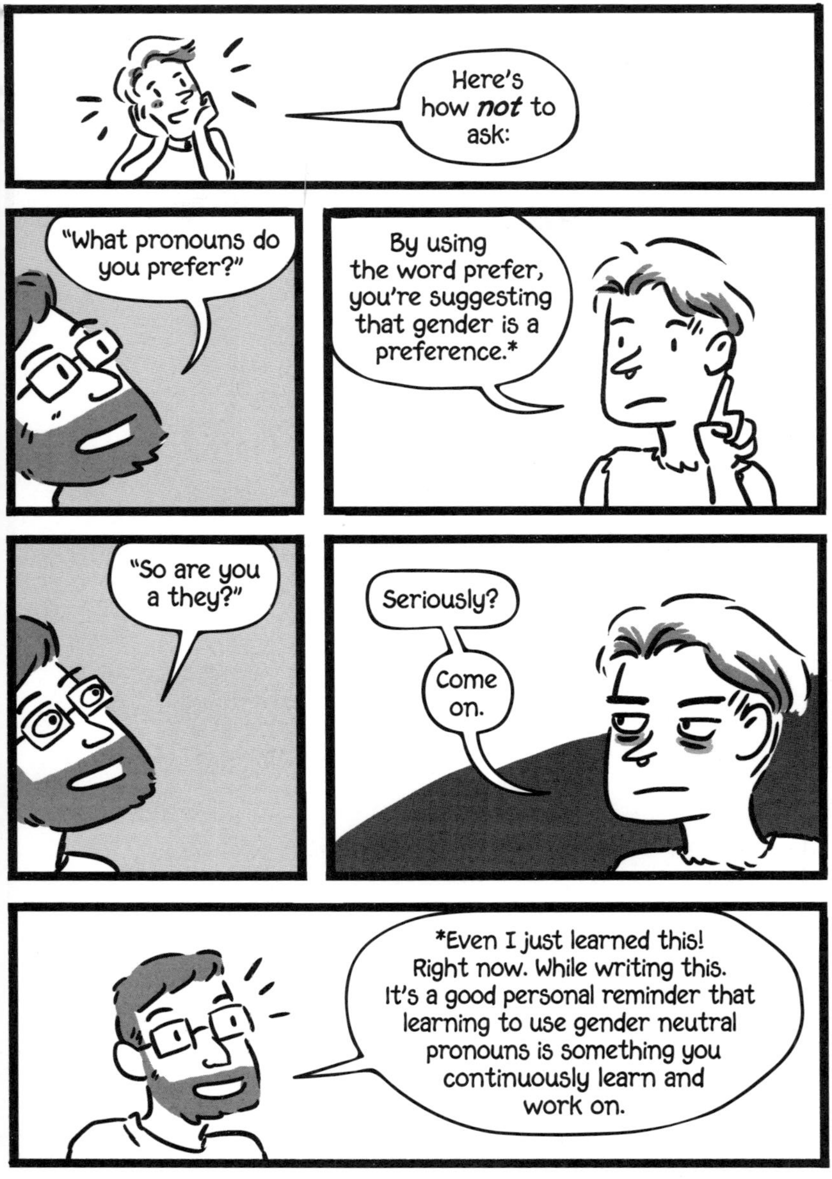
Here's how *not* to ask:
"What pronouns do you prefer?"
By using the word prefer, you're suggesting that gender is a preference.*
"So are you a they?"
Seriously?
Come on.
*Even I just learned this! Right now. While writing this. It's a good personal reminder that learning to use gender neutral pronouns is something you continuously learn and work on.

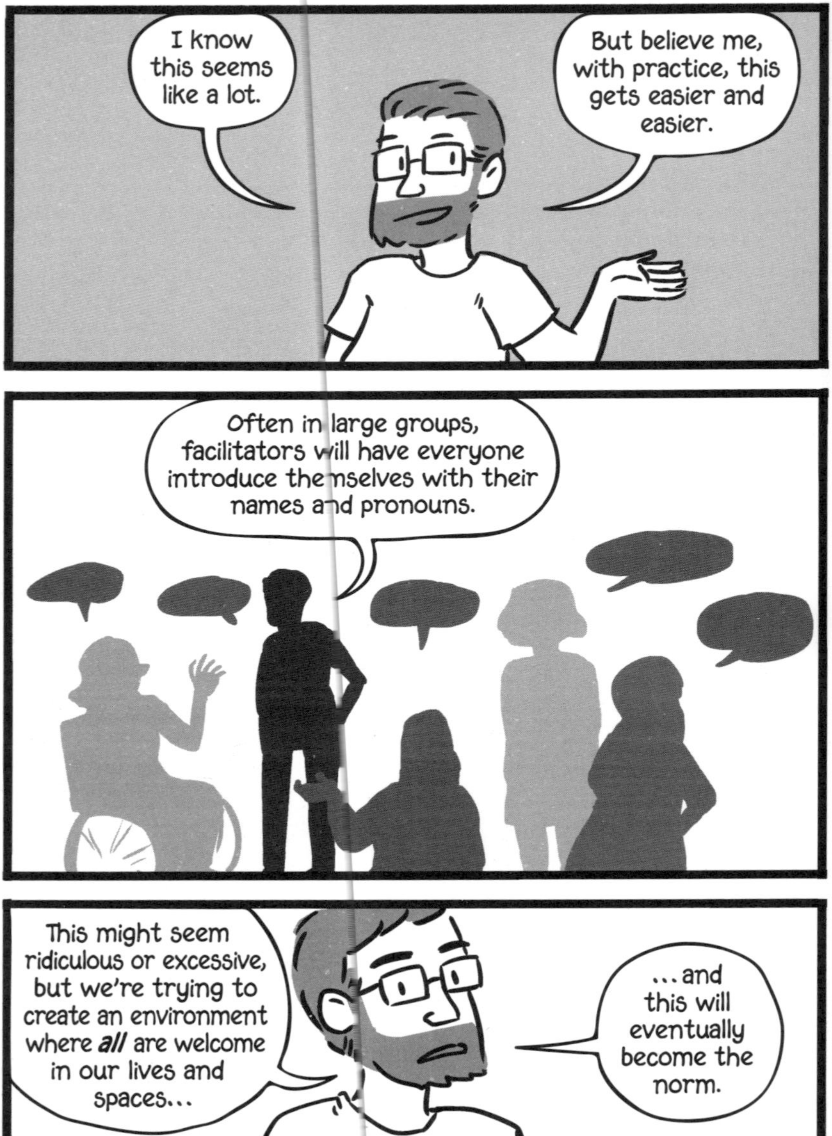

I know this seems like a lot.
But believe me, with practice, this gets easier and easier.
Often in large groups, facilitators will have everyone introduce themselves with their names and pronouns.
This might seem ridiculous or excessive, but we're trying to create an environment where *all* are welcome in our lives and spaces...
...and this will eventually become the norm.

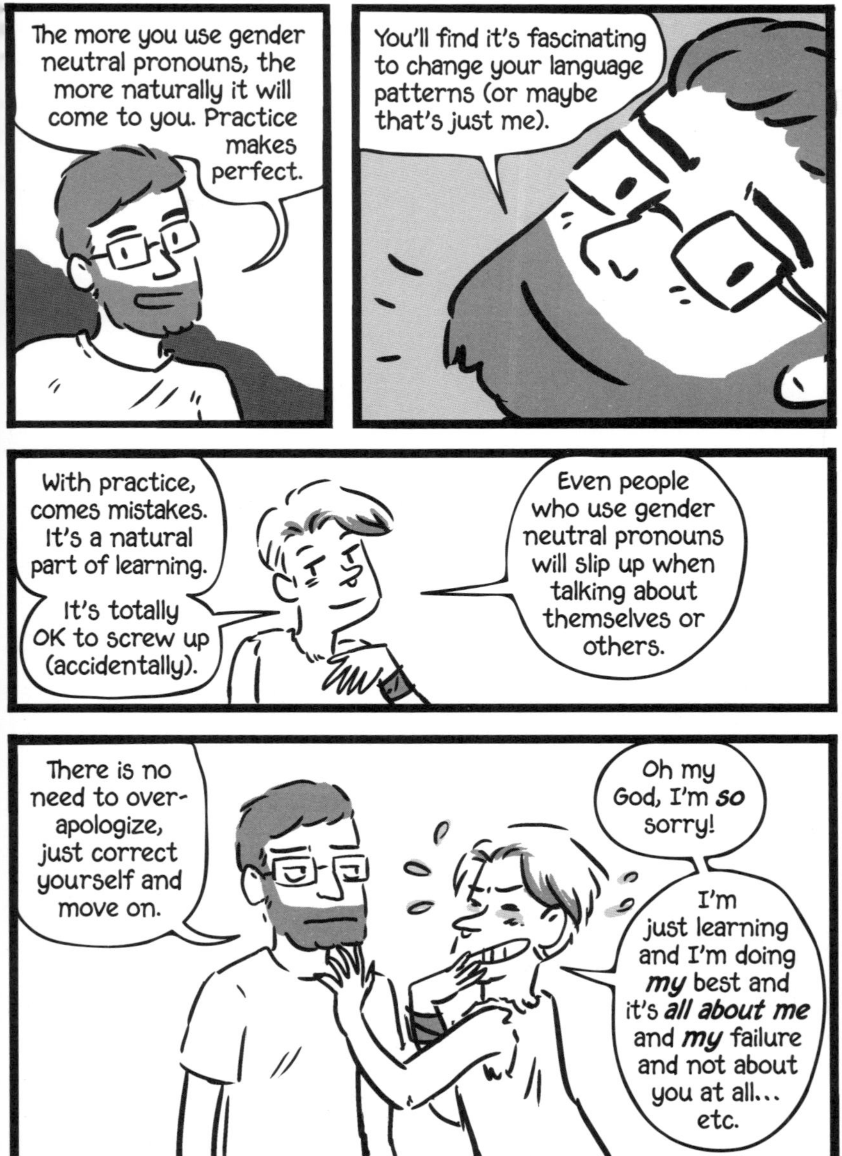
The more you use gender neutral pronouns, the more naturally it will come to you. Practice makes perfect.
You'll find it's fascinating to change your language patterns (or maybe that's just me).
With practice, comes mistakes. It's a natural part of learning.
It's totally OK to screw up (accidentally).
Even people who use gender neutral pronouns will slip up when talking about themselves or others.
There is no need to over-apologize, just correct yourself and move on.
Oh my God, I'm *so* sorry!
I'm just learning and I'm doing *my* best and it's *all about me* and *my* failure and not about you at all... etc.

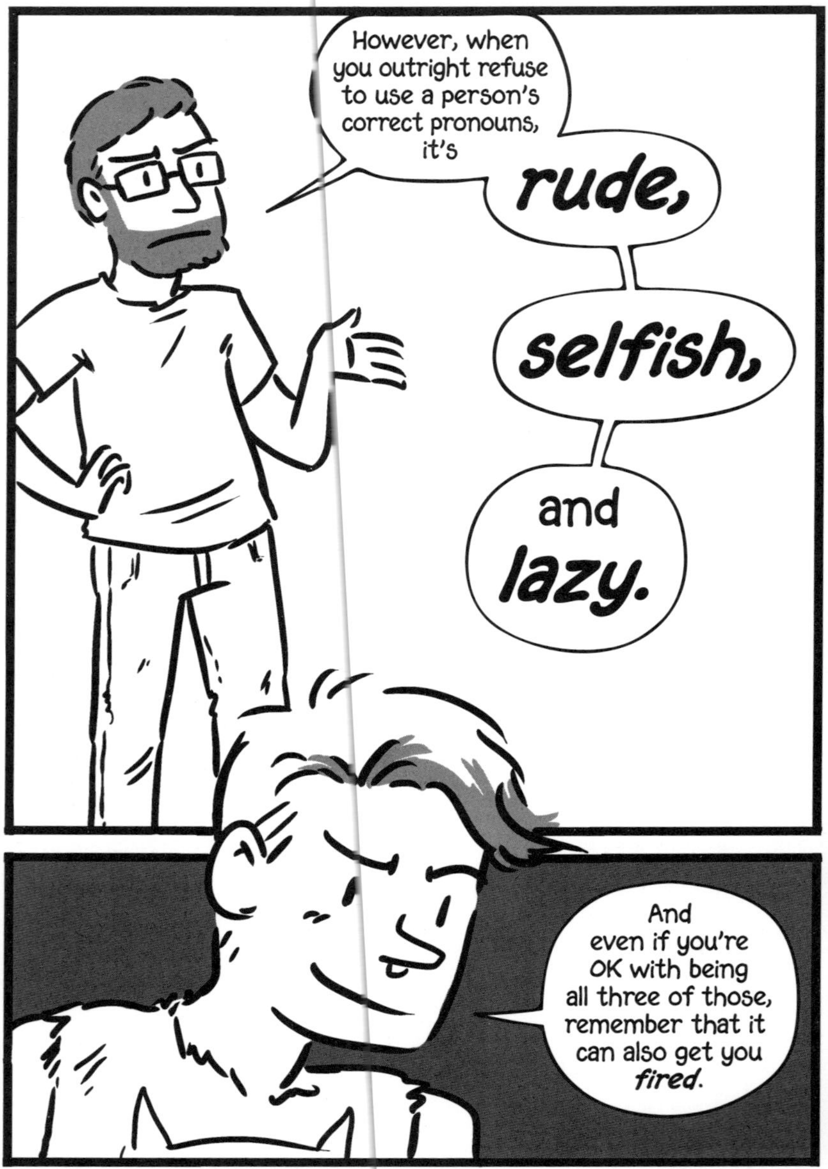
However, when you outright refuse to use a person's correct pronouns, it's
rude,
selfish,
and lazy.
And even if you're OK with being all three of those, remember that it can also get you fired.

How to use They/Them pronouns in a professional setting

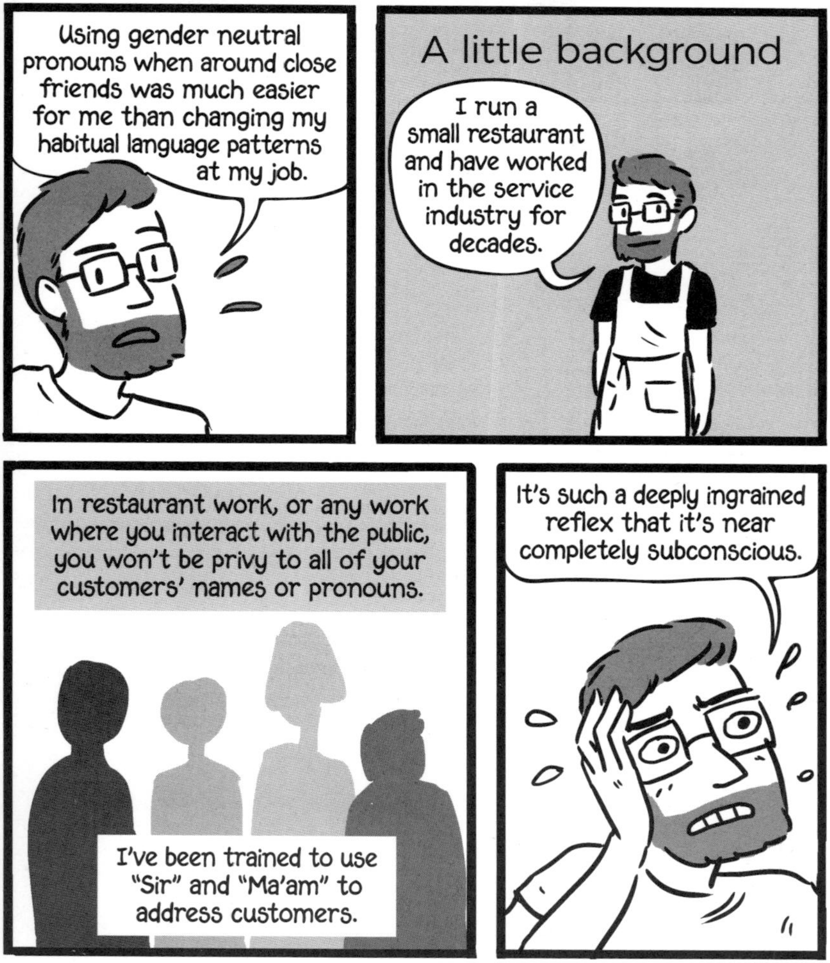
Using gender neutral pronouns when around close friends was much easier for me than changing my habitual language patterns at my job.
A little background
I run a small restaurant and have worked in the service industry for decades.
In restaurant work, or any work where you interact with the public, you won't be privy to all of your customers' names or pronouns.
I've been trained to use "Sir" and "Ma'am" to address customers.
It's such a deeply ingrained reflex that it's near completely subconscious.

It makes unlearning this language extremely challenging.

The only way to improve is with time and practice.

WAYS TO CHANGE YOUR LANGUAGE:

Hey guys/ Hey ladies	Hey y'all. Hello everyone. Hey folks.
Sir/Ma'am	Just remove them from the greeting, i.e.: "Hello, Sir" becomes "Hello."

When referring to a customer in the third person, learn to default to "they."

Instead of using gender as a descriptor, use their clothing or hair: "That person in the green shirt."

It will feel clunky at first, but remember that this work is hard but necessary.

Also, sorry to the hundreds of people I've accidentally misgendered while at work.

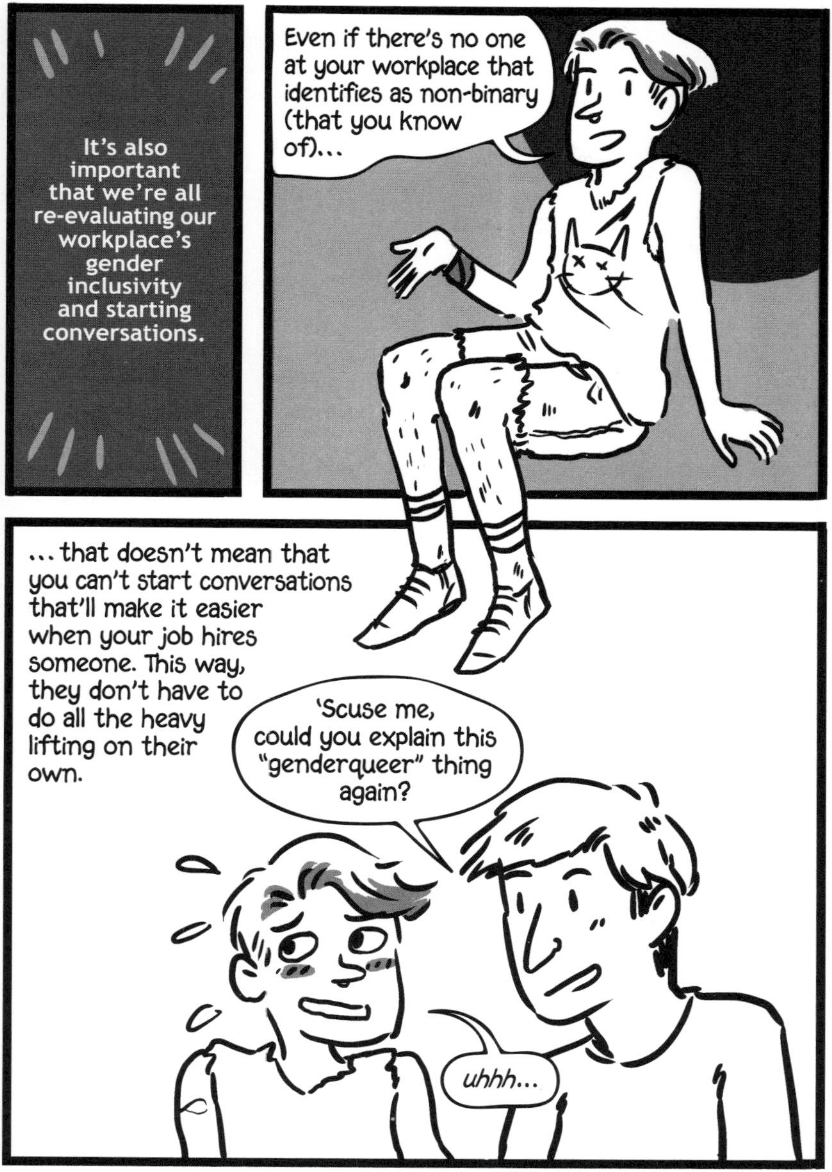

It's also important that we're all re-evaluating our workplace's gender inclusivity and starting conversations.
Even if there's no one at your workplace that identifies as non-binary (that you know of)...
...that doesn't mean that you can't start conversations that'll make it easier when your job hires someone. This way, they don't have to do all the heavy lifting on their own.
'Scuse me, could you explain this "genderqueer" thing again?
uhhh...

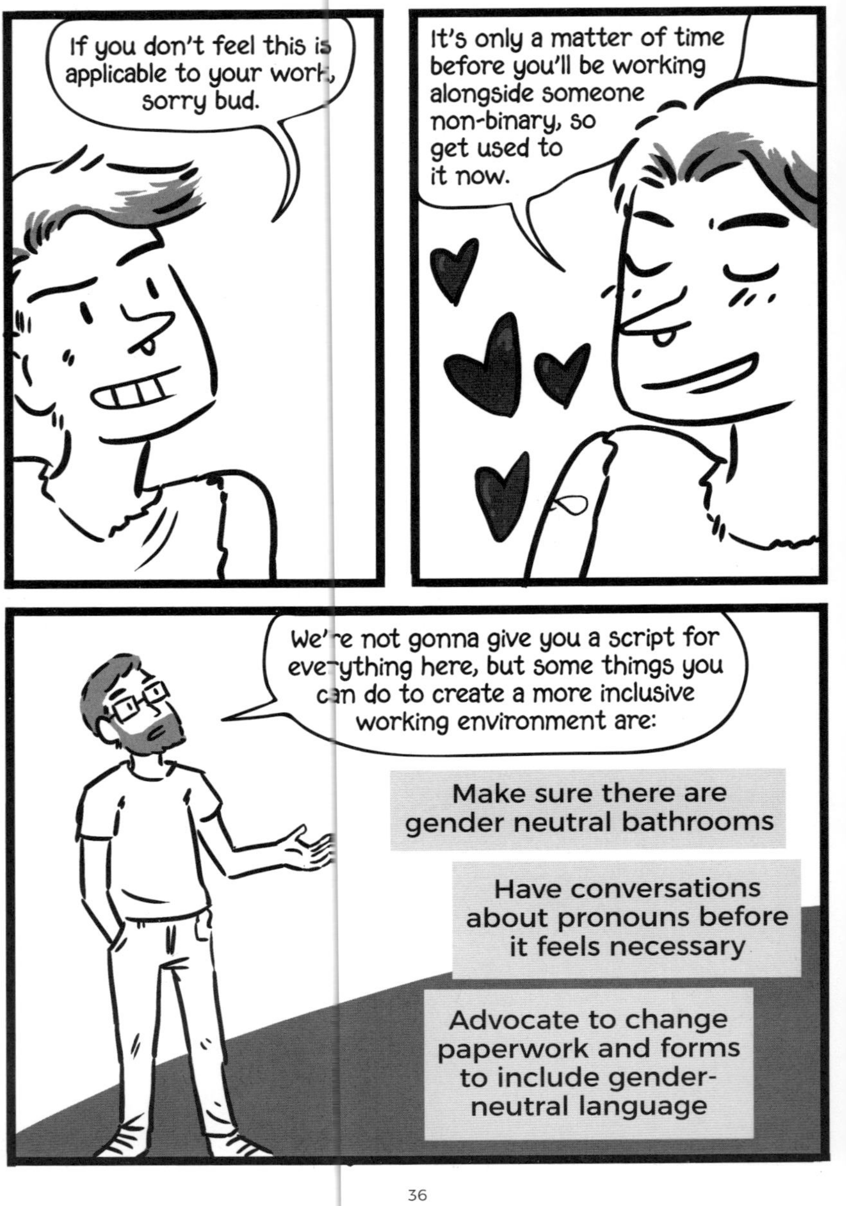
If you don't feel this is applicable to your work, sorry bud.
It's only a matter of time before you'll be working alongside someone non-binary, so get used to it now.
We're not gonna give you a script for everything here, but some things you can do to create a more inclusive working environment are:
Make sure there are gender neutral bathrooms
Have conversations about pronouns before it feels necessary
Advocate to change paperwork and forms to include gender-neutral language

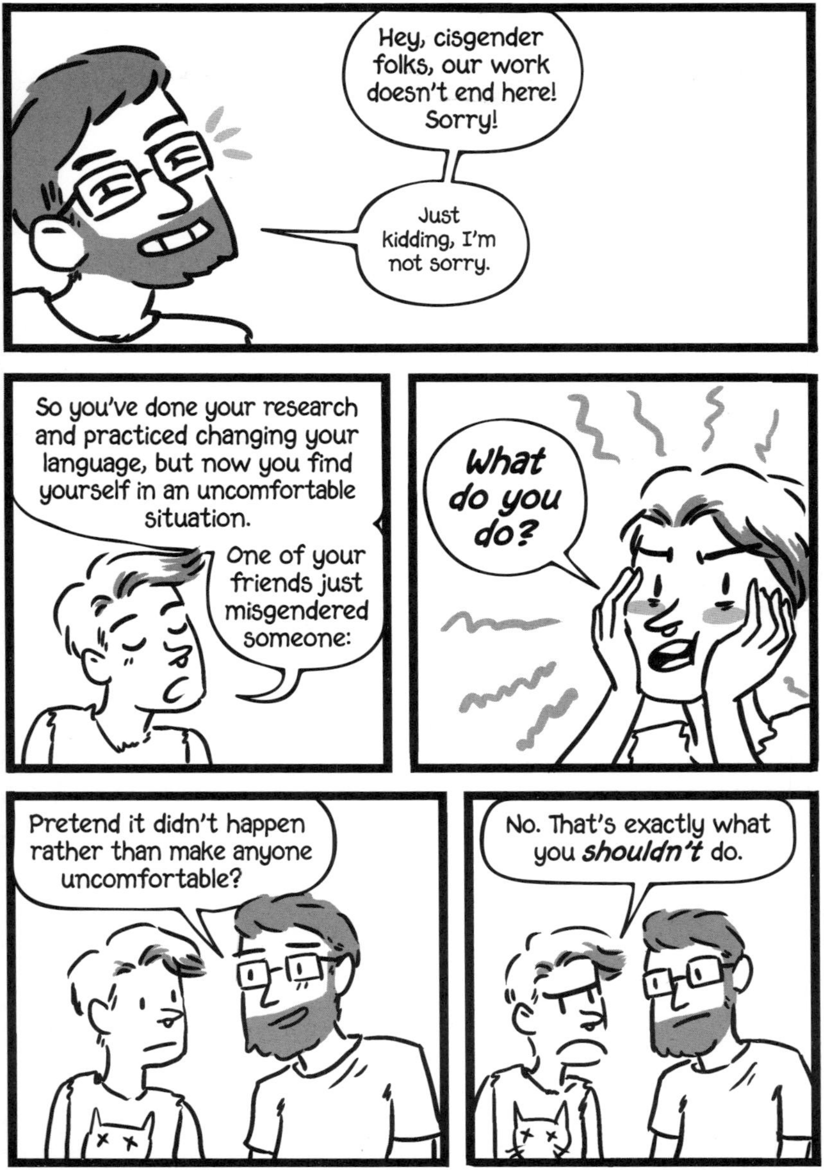
Hey, cisgender folks, our work doesn't end here! Sorry!
Just kidding, I'm not sorry.
So you've done your research and practiced changing your language, but now you find yourself in an uncomfortable situation.
One of your friends just misgendered someone:
What do you do?
Pretend it didn't happen rather than make anyone uncomfortable?
No. That's exactly what you *shouldn't* do.

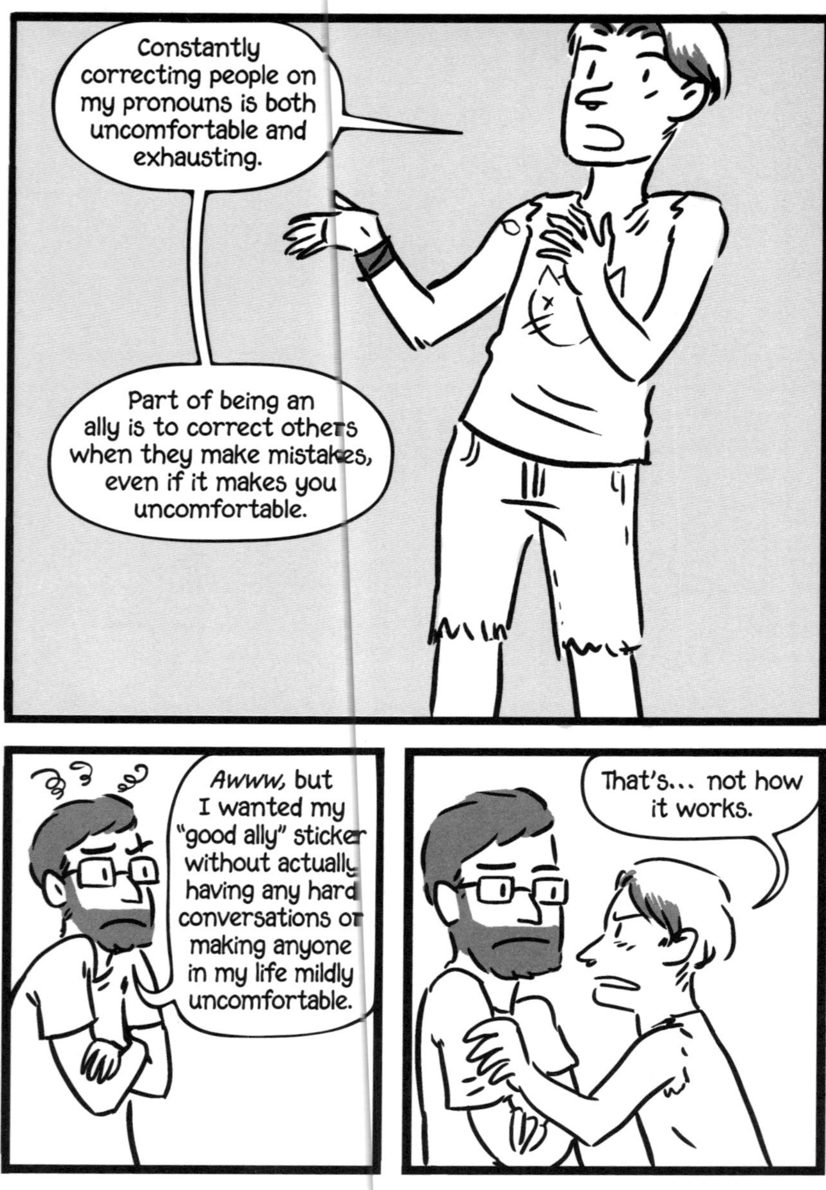
Constantly correcting people on my pronouns is both uncomfortable and exhausting.
Part of being an ally is to correct others when they make mistakes, even if it makes you uncomfortable.
Awww, but I wanted my "good ally" sticker without actually having any hard conversations or making anyone in my life mildly uncomfortable.
That's... not how it works.

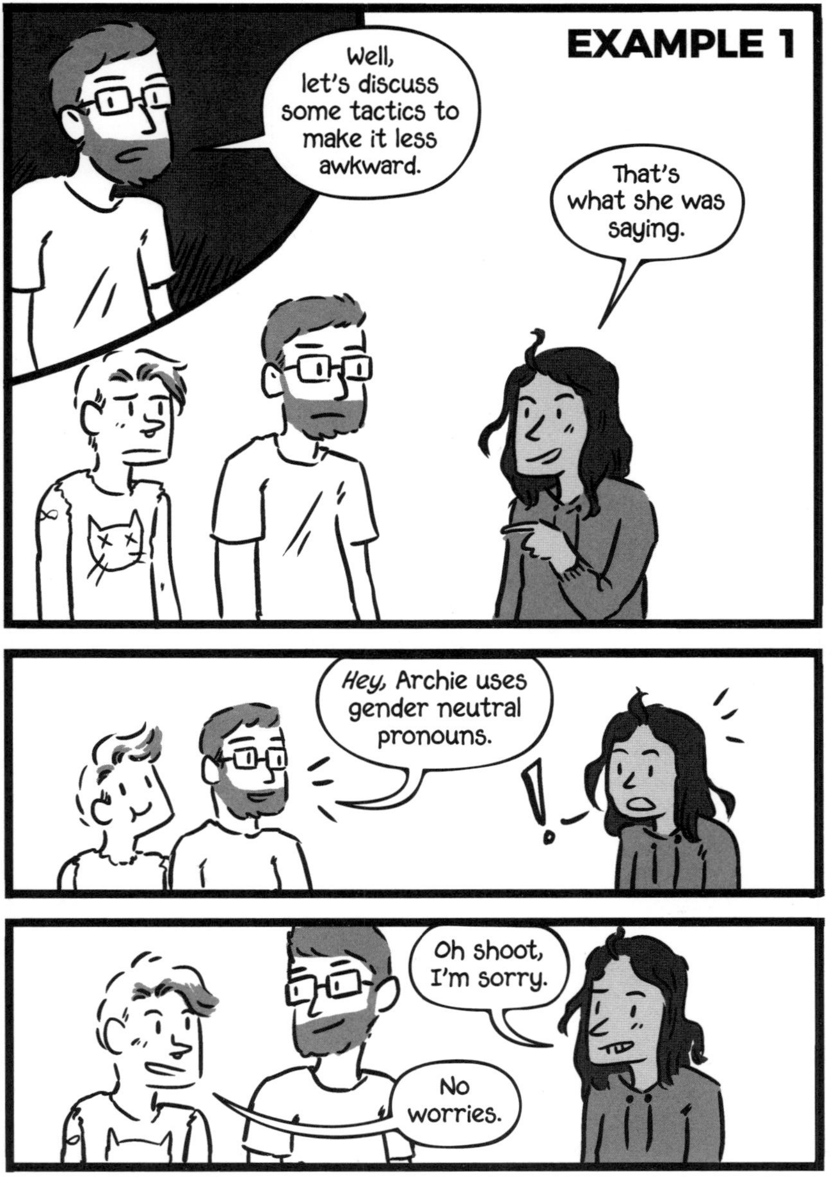
EXAMPLE 1
Well, let's discuss some tactics to make it less awkward.
That's what she was saying.
Hey, Archie uses gender neutral pronouns.
!
Oh shoot, I'm sorry.
No worries.

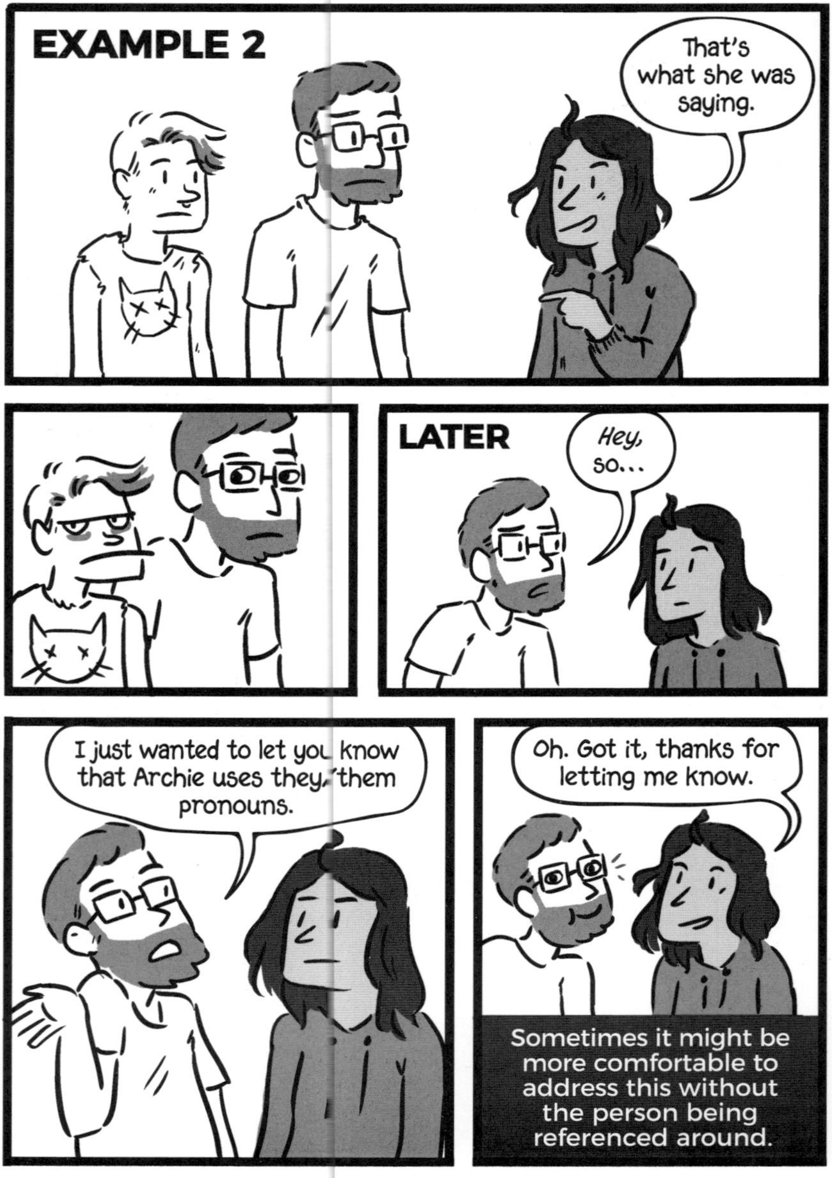
EXAMPLE 2
That's what she was saying.
LATER
Hey, so...
I just wanted to let you know that Archie uses they/them pronouns.
Oh. Got it, thanks for letting me know.
Sometimes it might be more comfortable to address this without the person being referenced around.

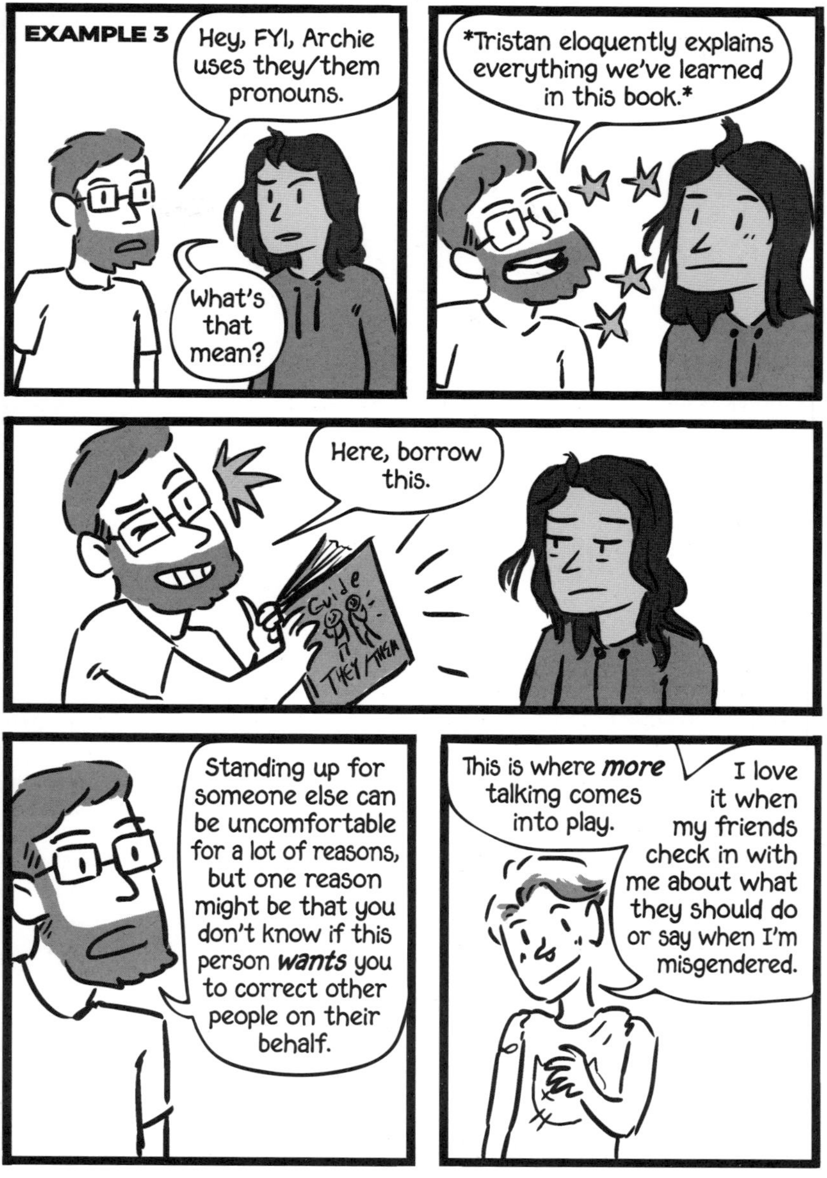
EXAMPLE 3
Hey, FYI, Archie uses they/them pronouns.
What's that mean?
Tristan eloquently explains everything we've learned in this book.
Here, borrow this.
Guide
THEY/THEM
Standing up for someone else can be uncomfortable for a lot of reasons, but one reason might be that you don't know if this person *wants* you to correct other people on their behalf.
This is where *more* talking comes into play.
I love it when my friends check in with me about what they should do or say when I'm misgendered.

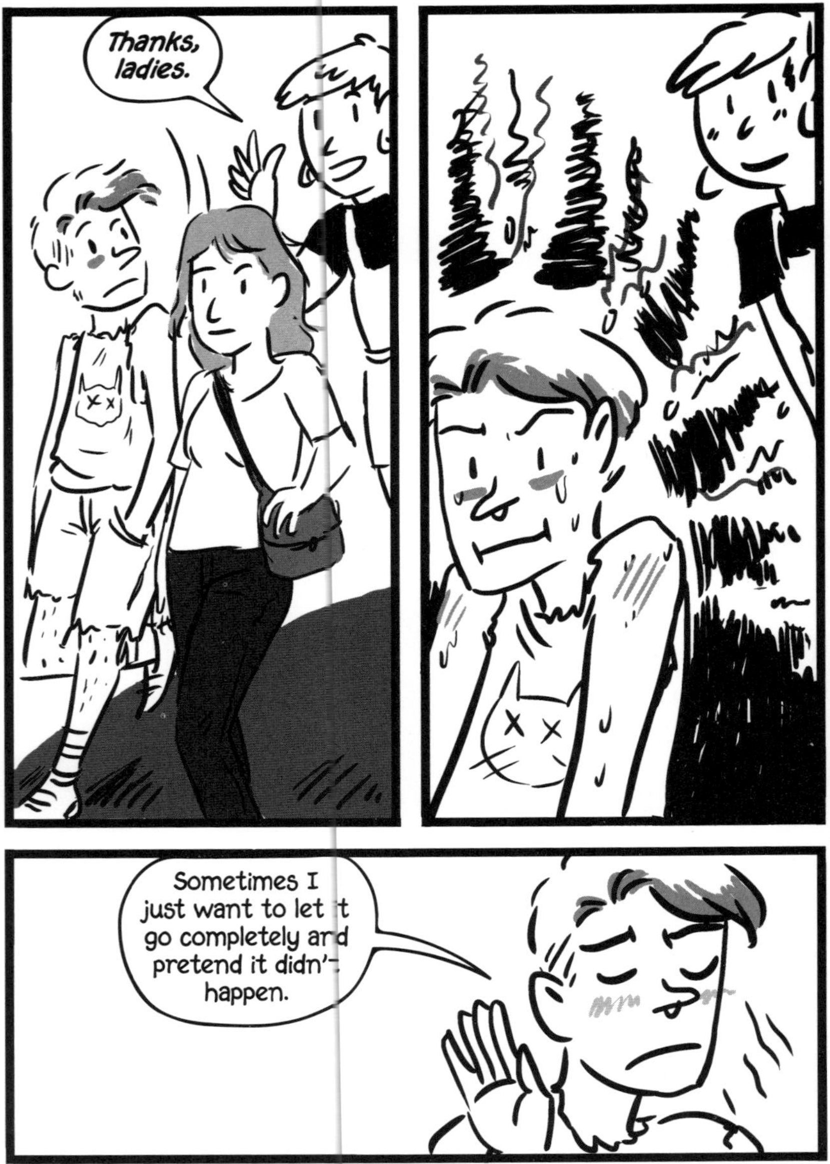
Thanks, ladies.
Sometimes I just want to let it go completely and pretend it didn't happen.

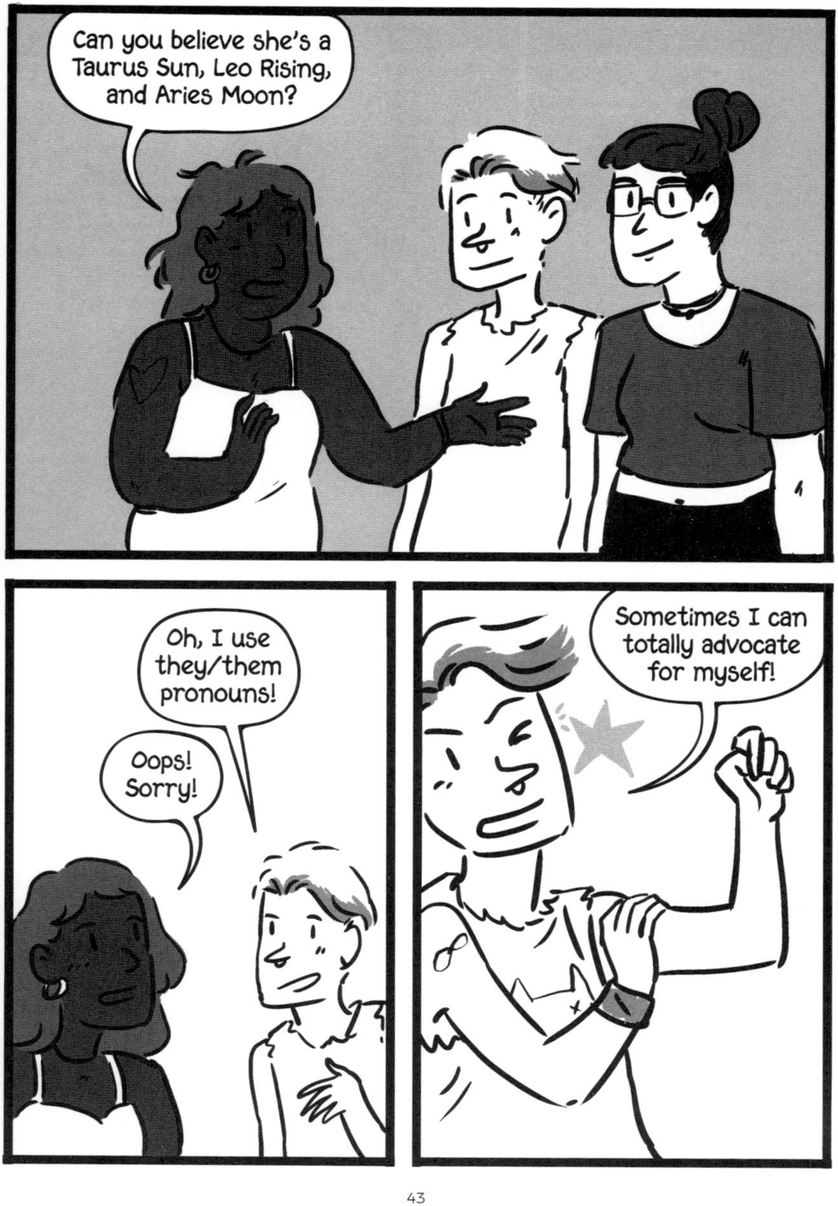
Can you believe she's a Taurus Sun, Leo Rising, and Aries Moon?
Oh, I use they/them pronouns!
Oops! Sorry!
Sometimes I can totally advocate for myself!

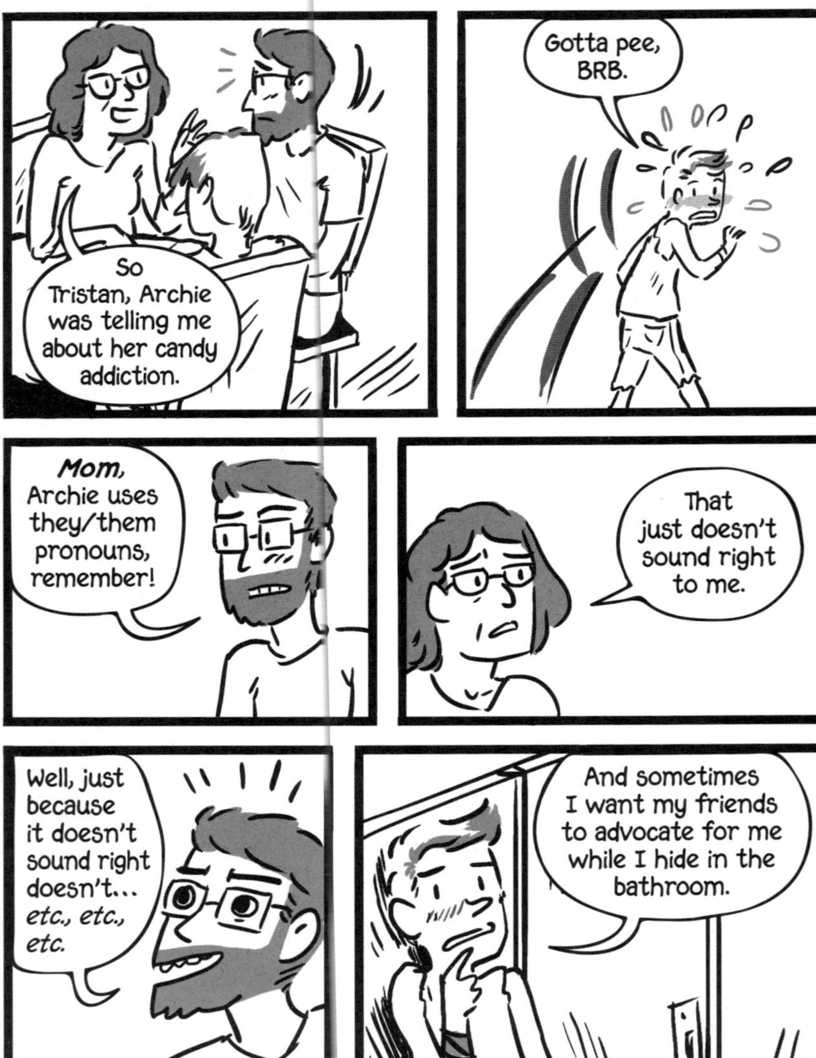
So Tristan, Archie was telling me about her candy addiction.
Gotta pee, BRB.
Mom, Archie uses they/them pronouns, remember!
That just doesn't sound right to me.
Well, just because it doesn't sound right doesn't... *etc., etc., etc.*
And sometimes I want my friends to advocate for me while I hide in the bathroom.
Like Archie said, the best way to know is to ask your friends and co-workers how they'd like you to handle the situation and follow their wishes.

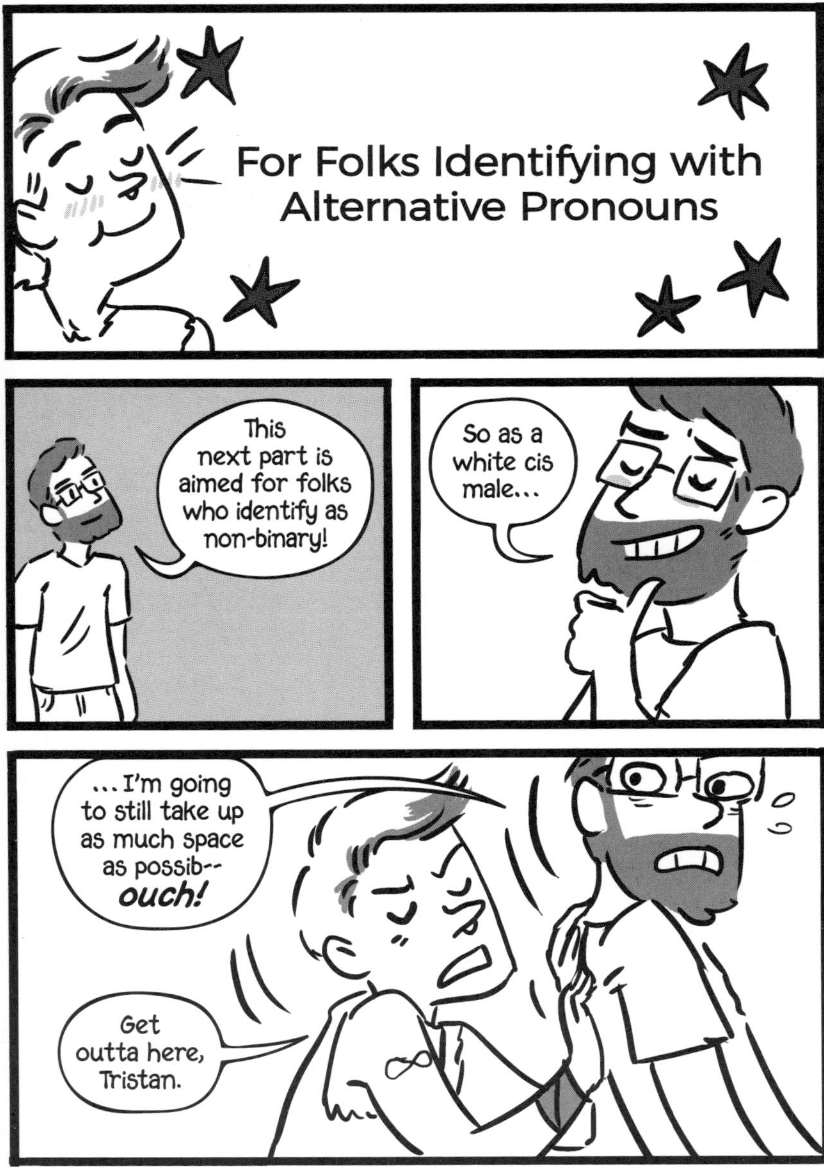
For Folks Identifying with Alternative Pronouns
This next part is aimed for folks who identify as non-binary!
So as a white cis male...
...I'm going to still take up as much space as possib-- ouch!
Get outta here, Tristan.

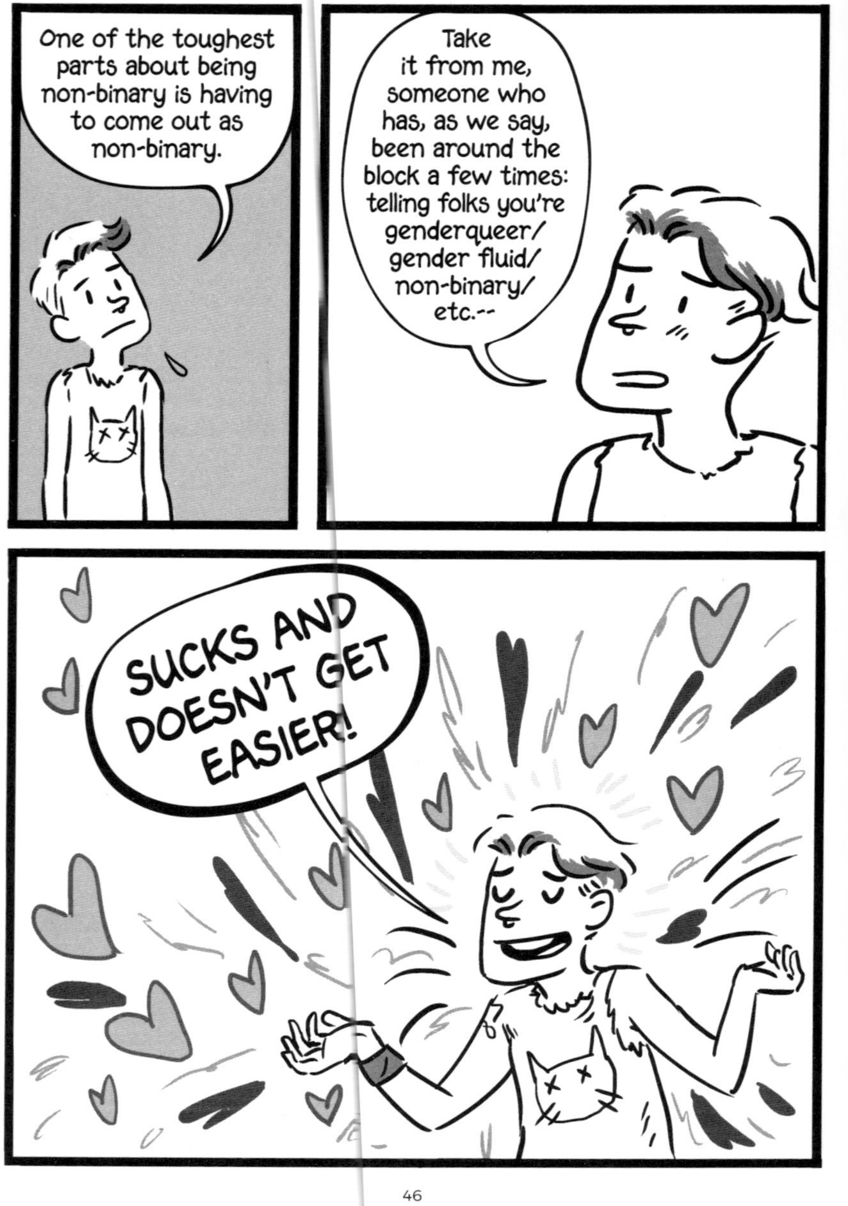
One of the toughest parts about being non-binary is having to come out as non-binary.
Take it from me, someone who has, as we say, been around the block a few times: telling folks you're genderqueer/ gender fluid/ non-binary/ etc.--
SUCKS AND DOESN'T GET EASIER!

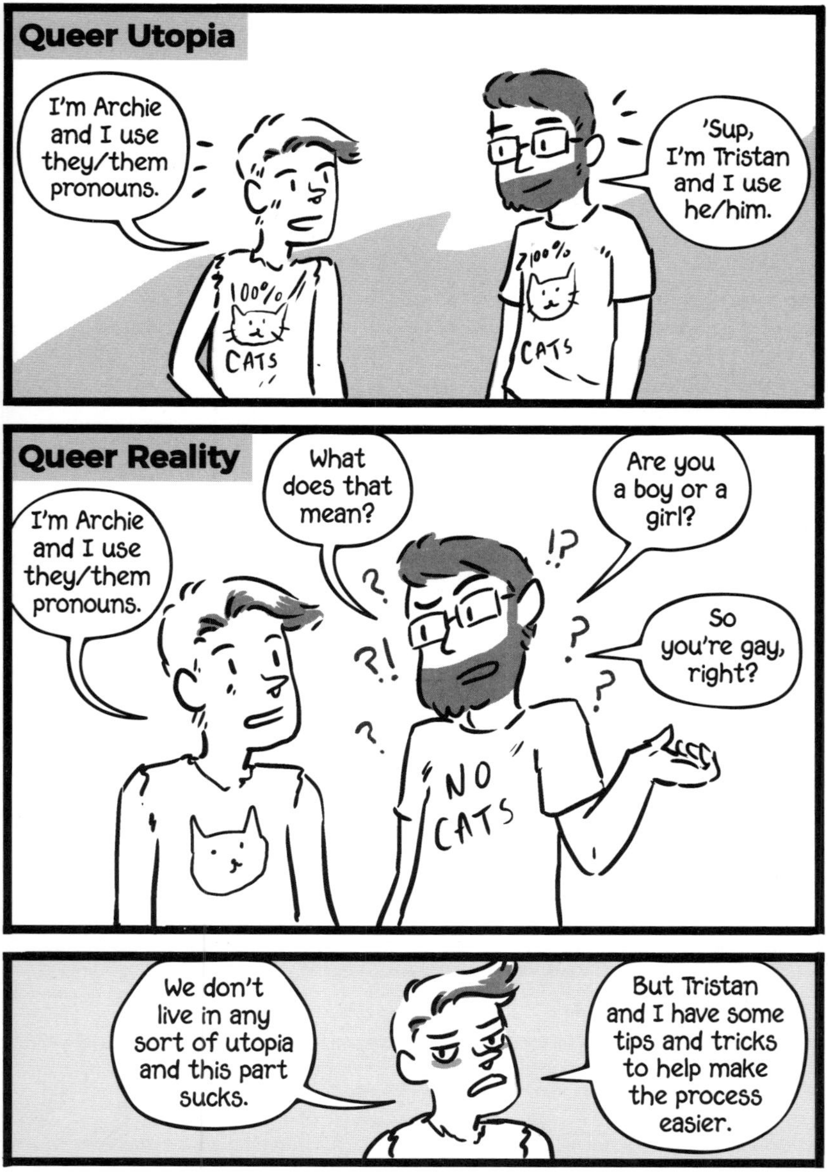

Queer Utopia
I'm Archie and I use they/them pronouns.
'Sup, I'm Tristan and I use he/him.
100% CATS
100% CATS
Queer Reality
I'm Archie and I use they/them pronouns.
What does that mean?
Are you a boy or a girl?
So you're gay, right?
NO CATS
We don't live in any sort of utopia and this part sucks.
But Tristan and I have some tips and tricks to help make the process easier.

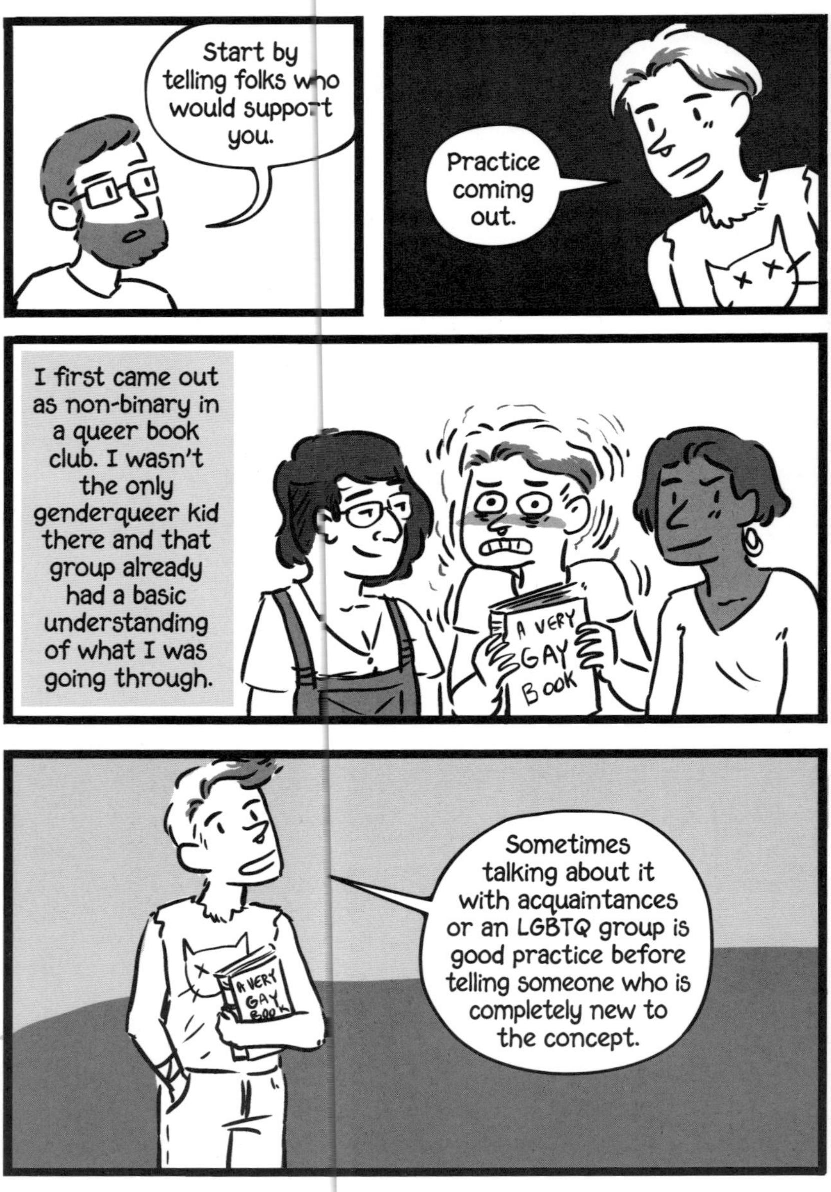
Start by telling folks who would support you.
Practice coming out.
I first came out as non-binary in a queer book club. I wasn't the only genderqueer kid there and that group already had a basic understanding of what I was going through.
A VERY GAY BOOK
Sometimes talking about it with acquaintances or an LGBTQ group is good practice before telling someone who is completely new to the concept.

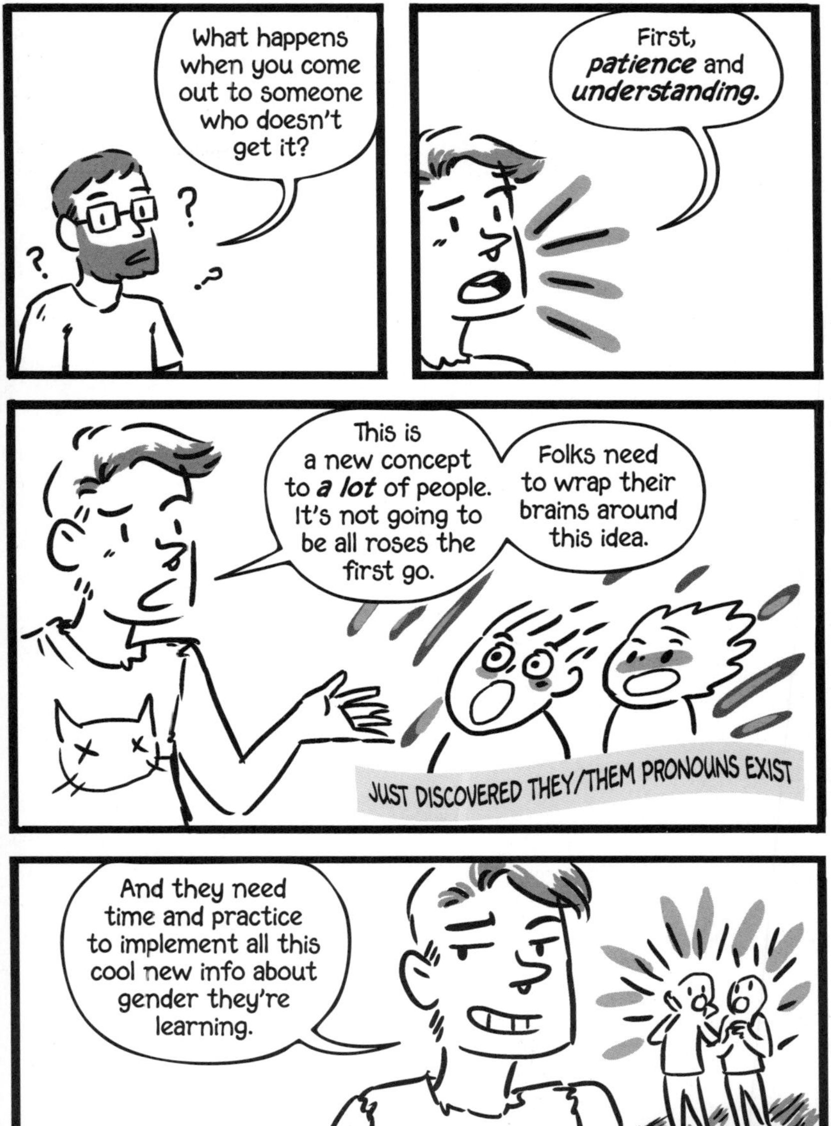
What happens when you come out to someone who doesn't get it?
First, *patience* and *understanding.*
This is a new concept to *a lot* of people. It's not going to be all roses the first go.
Folks need to wrap their brains around this idea.
JUST DISCOVERED THEY/THEM PRONOUNS EXIST
And they need time and practice to implement all this cool new info about gender they're learning.

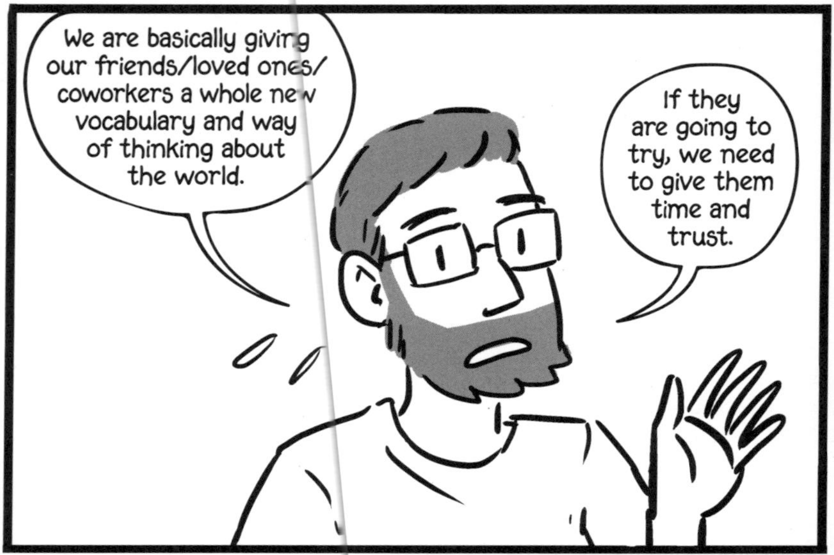
We are basically giving our friends/loved ones/ coworkers a whole new vocabulary and way of thinking about the world.
If they are going to try, we need to give them time and trust.

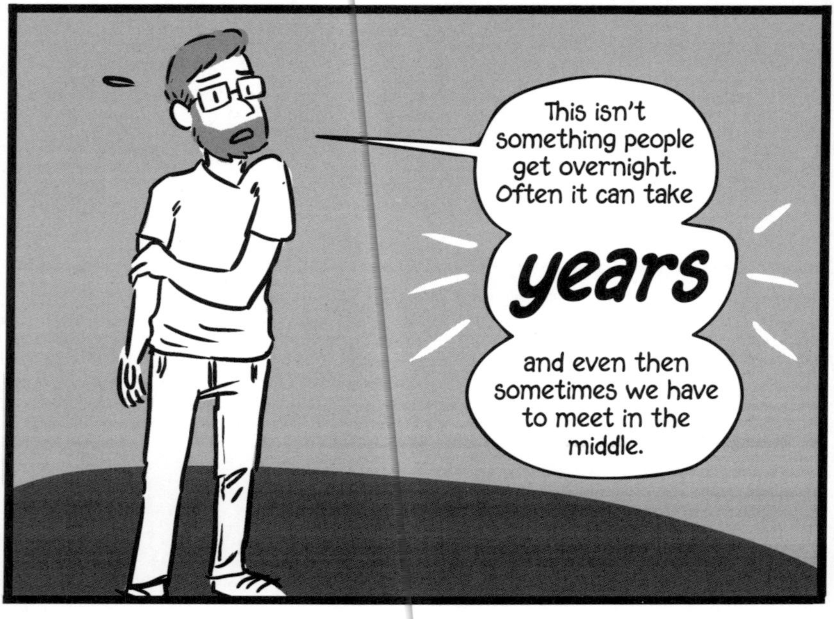
This isn't something people get overnight. Often it can take
years
and even then sometimes we have to meet in the middle.

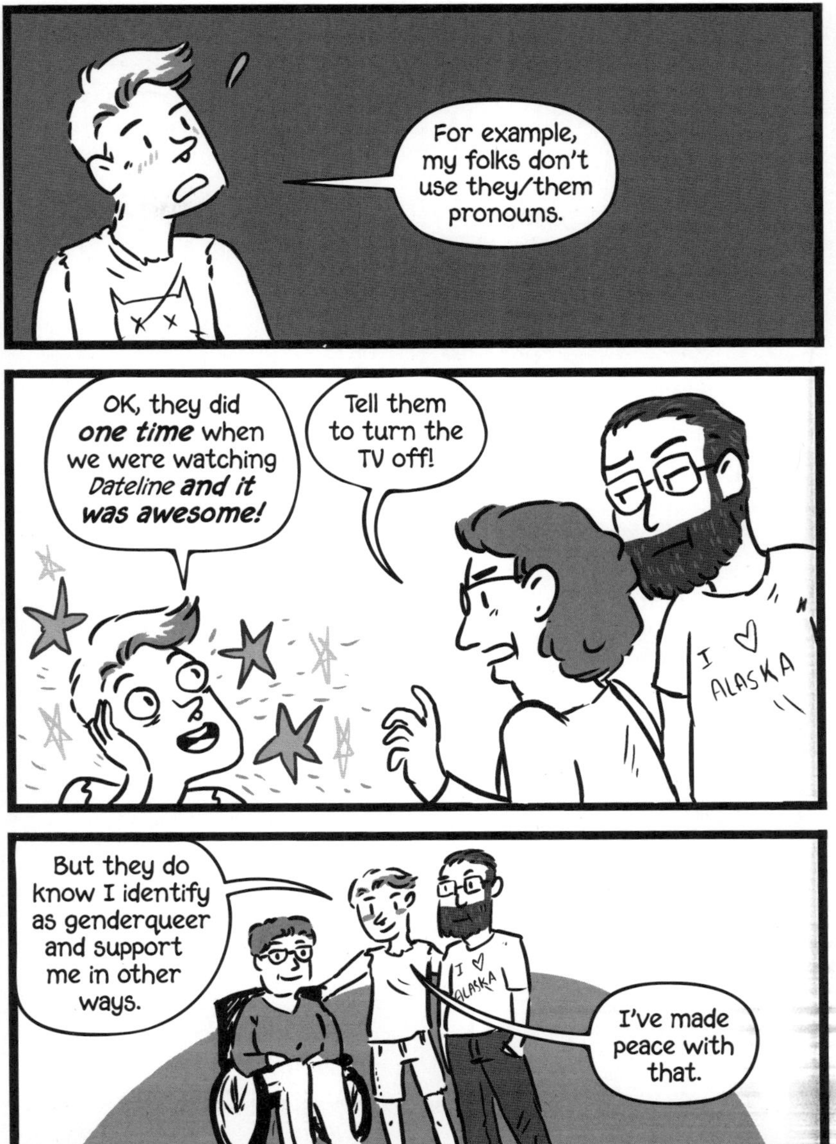
For example, my folks don't use they/them pronouns.
OK, they did **one time** when we were watching *Dateline* **and it was awesome!**
Tell them to turn the TV off!
I ♡ ALASKA
But they do know I identify as genderqueer and support me in other ways.
I ♡ ALASKA
I've made peace with that.

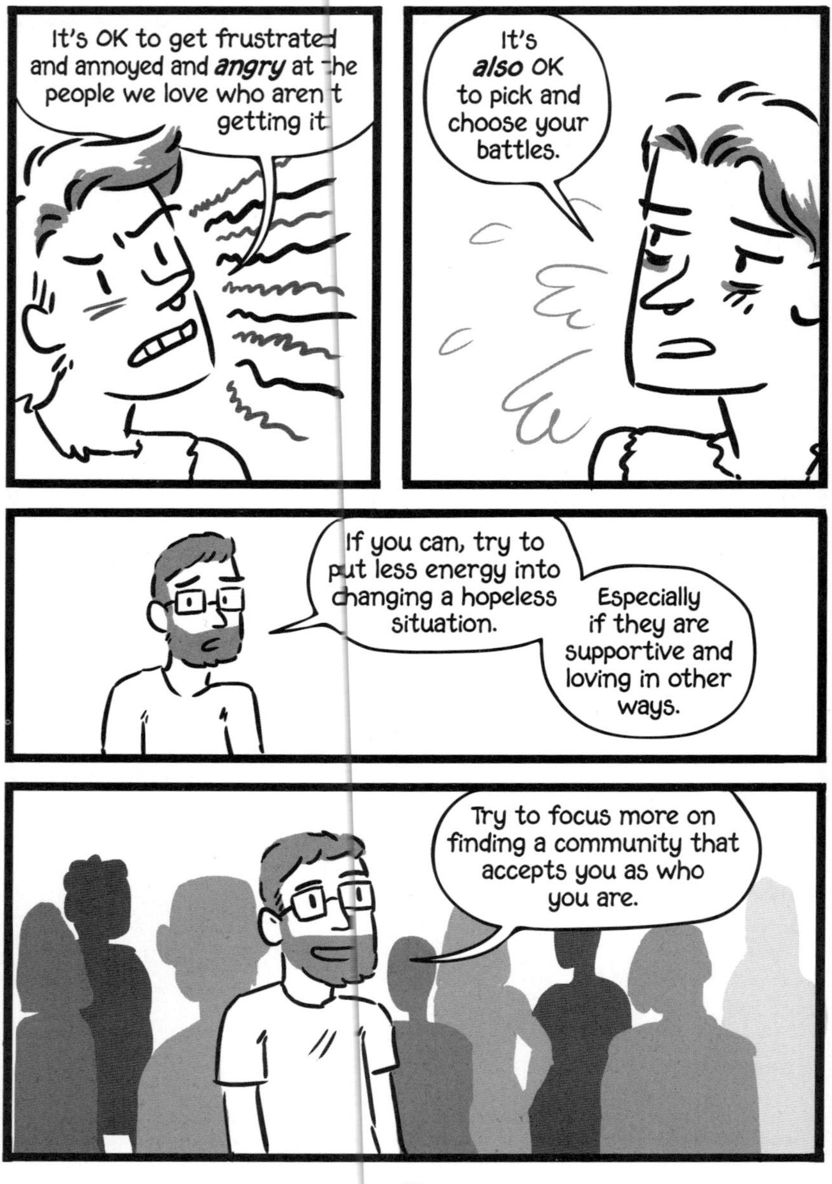
It's OK to get frustrated and annoyed and *angry* at the people we love who aren't getting it
It's *also* OK to pick and choose your battles.
If you can, try to put less energy into changing a hopeless situation.
Especially if they are supportive and loving in other ways.
Try to focus more on finding a community that accepts you as who you are.

For example, while I might not get the validation I want from my family...
...I've found groups (online and off) that accept me as who I am.
Folks I can vent to when it feels rough...
...and other non-binary folks I can exchange validation with.

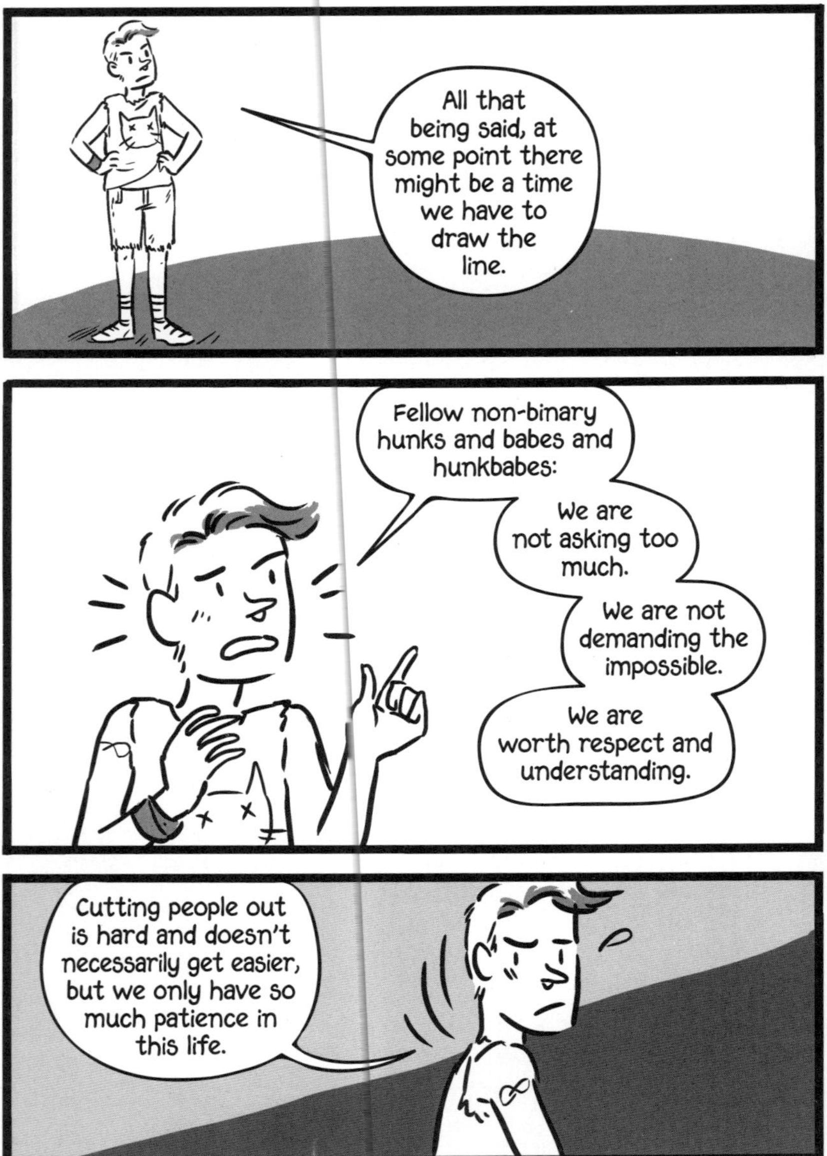
All that being said, at some point there might be a time we have to draw the line.
Fellow non-binary hunks and babes and hunkbabes:
We are not asking too much.
We are not demanding the impossible.
We are worth respect and understanding.
Cutting people out is hard and doesn't necessarily get easier, but we only have so much patience in this life.

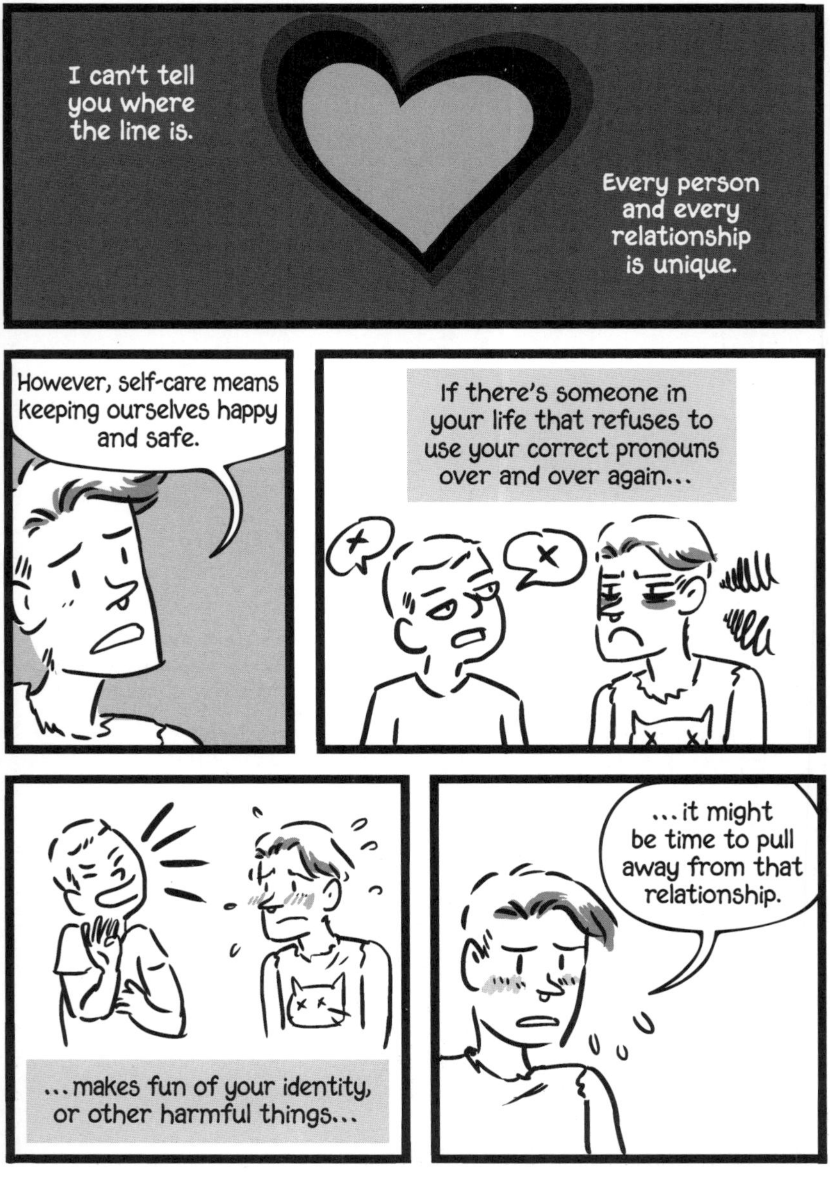

I can't tell you where the line is.
Every person and every relationship is unique.
However, self-care means keeping ourselves happy and safe.
If there's someone in your life that refuses to use your correct pronouns over and over again...
...makes fun of your identity, or other harmful things...
...it might be time to pull away from that relationship.

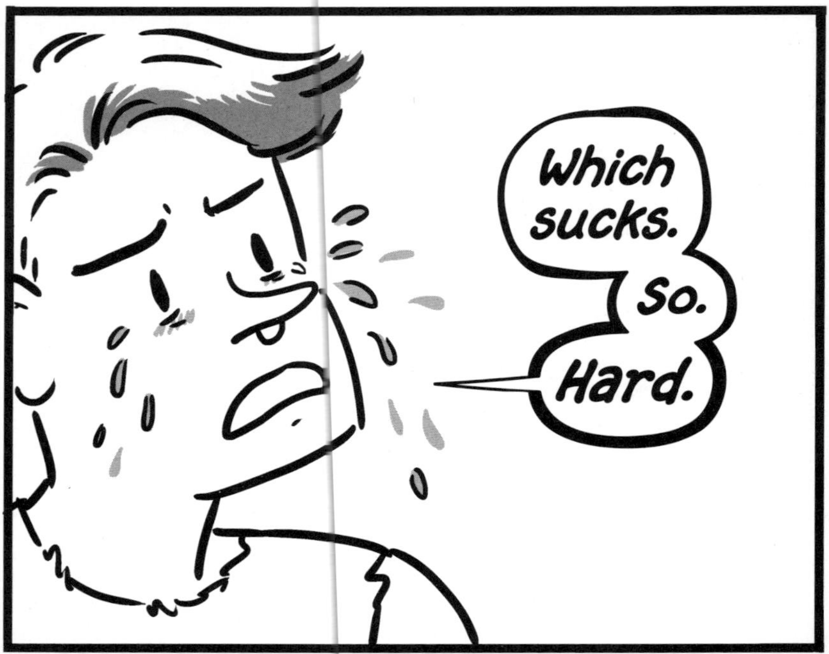
Which sucks.
So.
Hard.

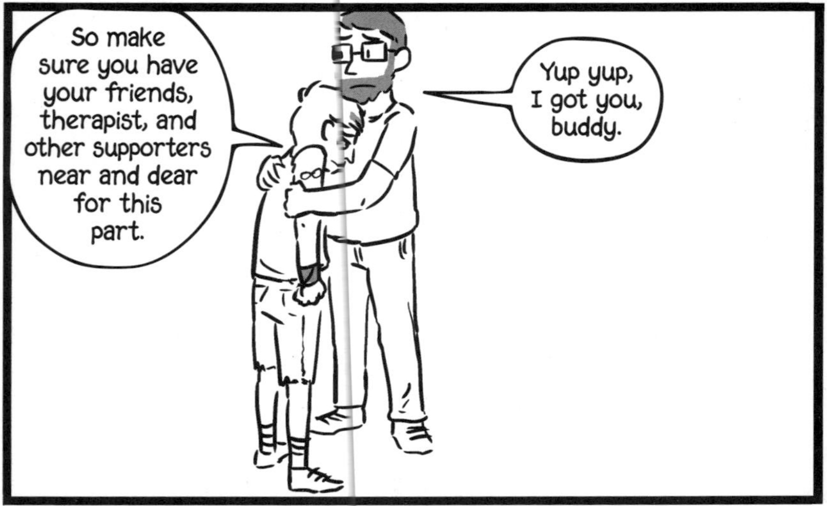
So make sure you have your friends, therapist, and other supporters near and dear for this part.
Yup yup, I got you, buddy.

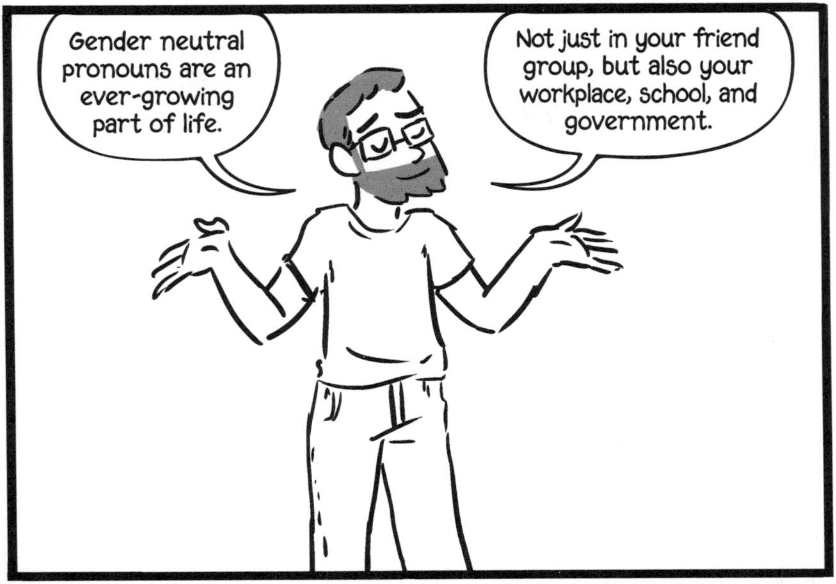
Gender neutral pronouns are an ever-growing part of life.
Not just in your friend group, but also your workplace, school, and government.

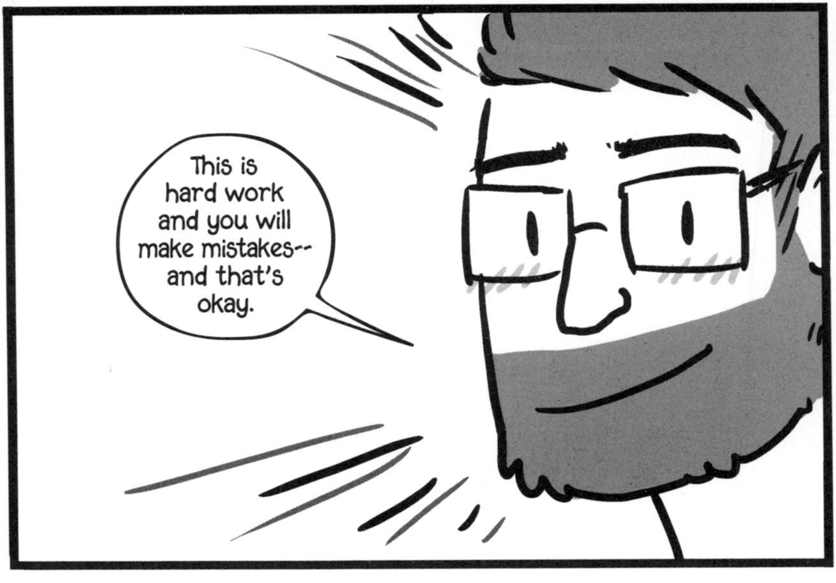
This is hard work and you will make mistakes--and that's okay.

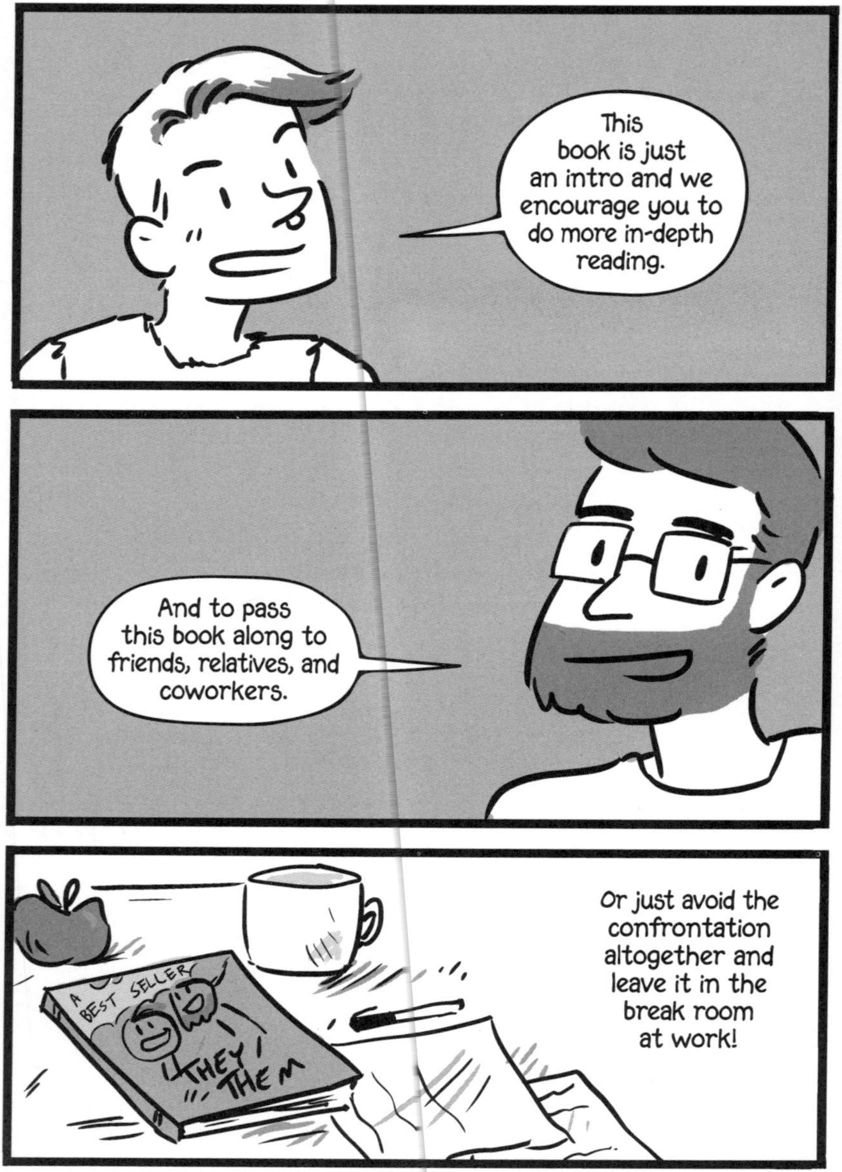
This book is just an intro and we encourage you to do more in-depth reading.
And to pass this book along to friends, relatives, and coworkers.
A BEST SELLER
THEY THEM
Or just avoid the confrontation altogether and leave it in the break room at work!

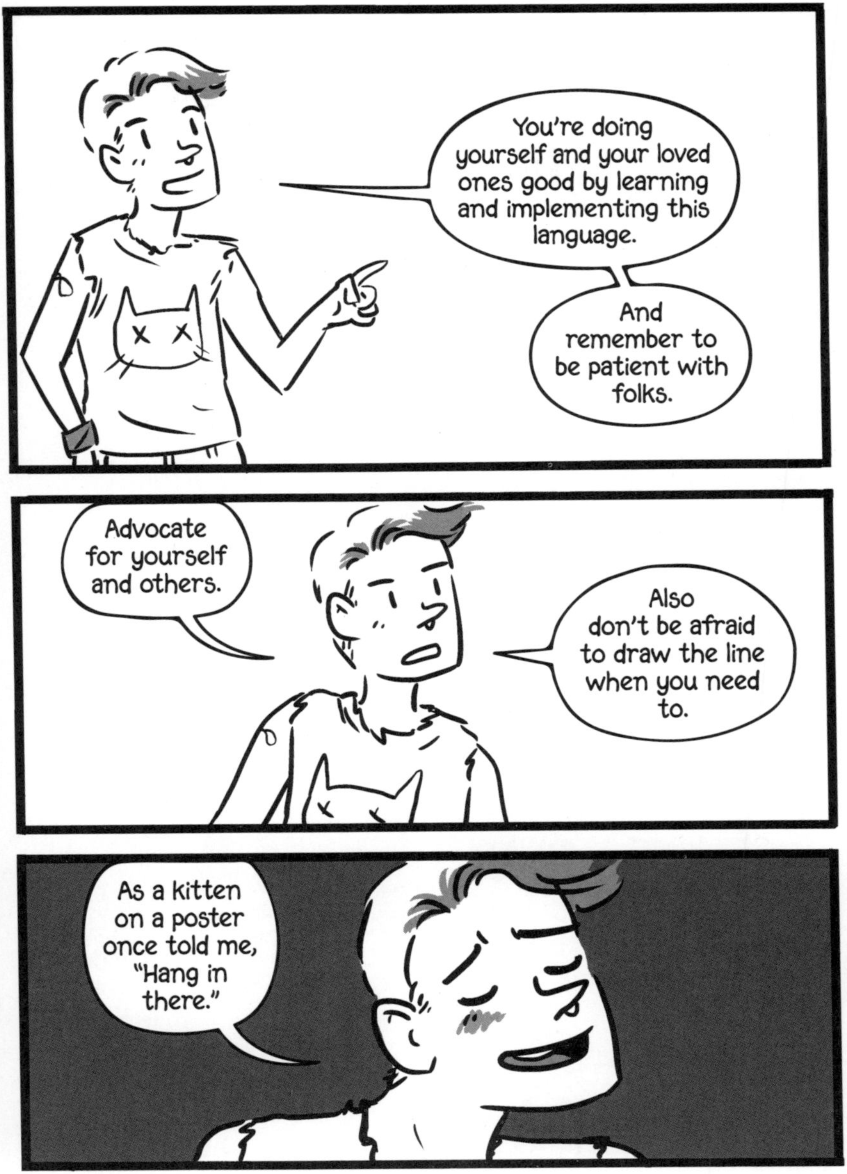
You're doing yourself and your loved ones good by learning and implementing this language.
And remember to be patient with folks.
Advocate for yourself and others.
Also don't be afraid to draw the line when you need to.
As a kitten on a poster once told me, "Hang in there."

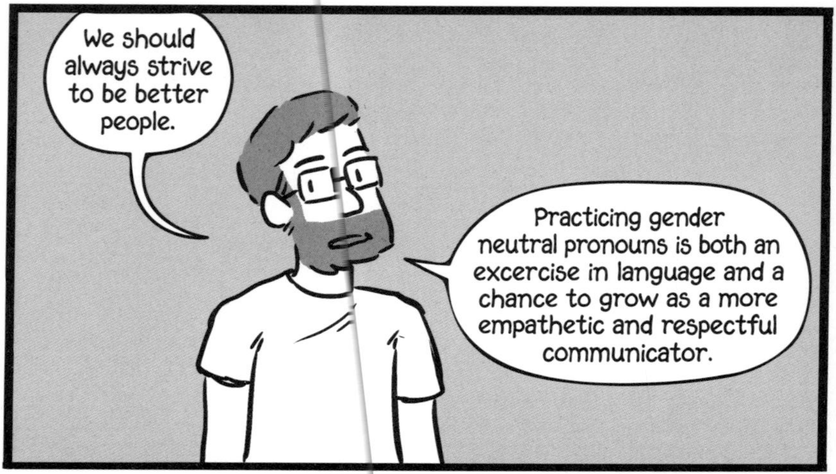
We should always strive to be better people.
Practicing gender neutral pronouns is both an excercise in language and a chance to grow as a more empathetic and respectful communicator.

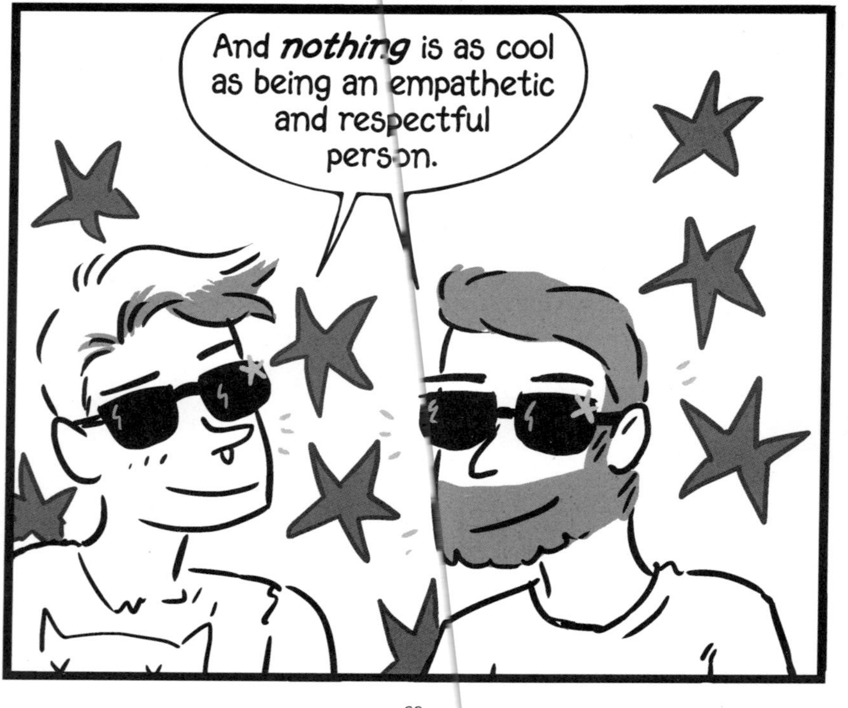
And *nothing* is as cool as being an empathetic and respectful person.

Quick and Easy Pronoun Reference Chart

Subject	Object	Possessive determiner	Possessive pronoun	Reflexive
She	Her	Her	Hers	Herself
He	Him	His	His	Himself
They	Them	Their	Theirs	Themself
Ze	Hir	Hir	Hirs	Hirself
Carol	Carol	Carol's	Carol's	Carol

He/She went to the store.

It belongs to him/her.

He said so himself/
She said so herself.

They went to the store.

It belongs to them.

They said so themself/
themselves.

Quick and Easy Scripts For When You Don't Know What To Say

How To Ask About Someone's Pronouns

"Hi, I'm ____ and I use ____ pronouns, what about you?"

"What pronouns do you all use?"

"Let's all go around and say our names and pronouns."

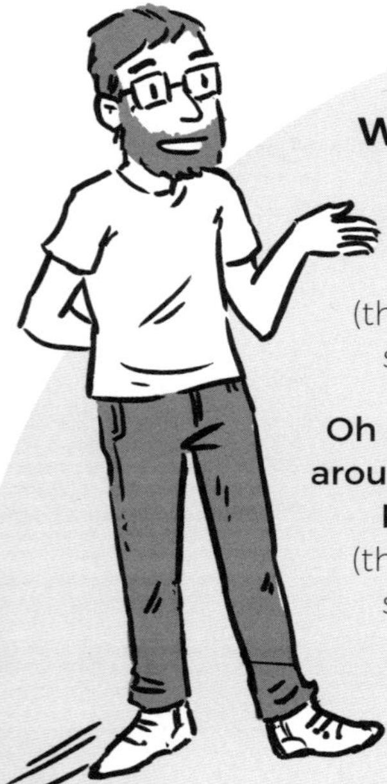

What To Say When You Mess Up Someone's Pronouns

Oops, I'm sorry.
(then carrying on with whatever you were saying but with the correct pronouns)

Oh shoot, sorry, I'm still wrapping my head around all of this but I'm going to get better. Please correct me if I mess up again.
(then carrying on with whatever you were saying but with the correct pronouns)

Quick and Easy Ideas For Using Gender Neutral Language

GENDERED	NON-GENDERED
Ladies/Gentlemen	Folks, Guests, Y'all
Men and Women	You all, Friends
Guys/Gals	Everyone, Anyone
The lady in that cool wolf shirt	The person in that cool wolf shirt

A Sample Sign You Could Post At Your Place Of Business

Please use gender-neutral language when addressing our staff.
Thanks for being a pal!

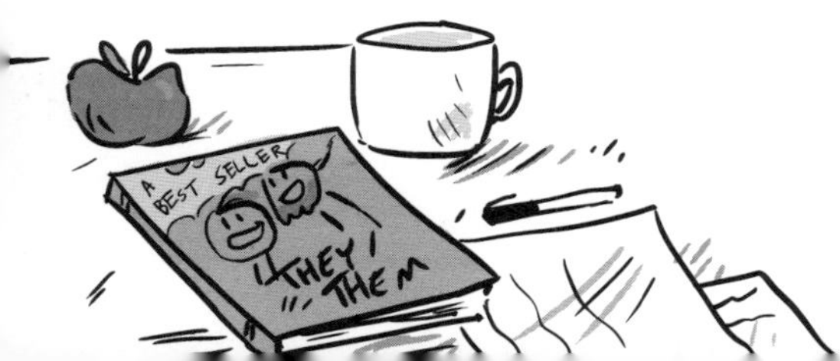
A BEST SELLER
THEY/THEM

Archie Bongiovanni has been drawing comics for over a decade, which also means that they're a part-time server. They've published monthly comics on *Autostraddle*, and have also drawn for *The Nib* and *Everyday Feminism*. They publish a lot of work from their own printer. They also teach comic courses to high schoolers at a local library, run a huge queer book club, and work at a feminist-owned sex shop. They will always eat the entire bag of Doritos in one sitting.

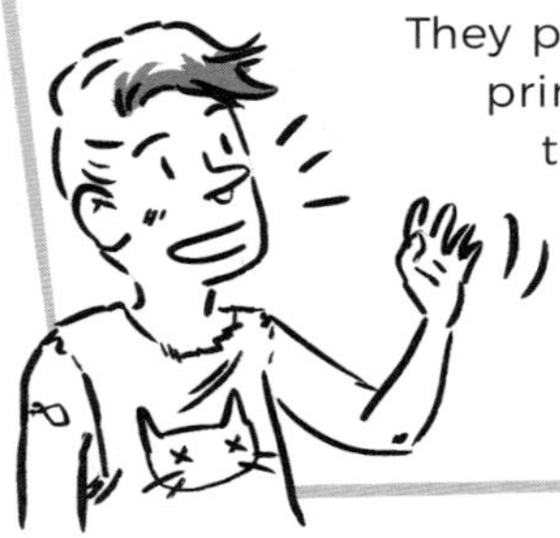

Tristan Jimerson has fumbled through a variety of careers and now runs a small restaurant. His work has been featured on *The Moth*, *NPR*, and zines that you find in the free bin at your local independent bookstore. He has the mind and body of a 30-year-old and the knees of a 55-year-old. He is tired almost all of the time.

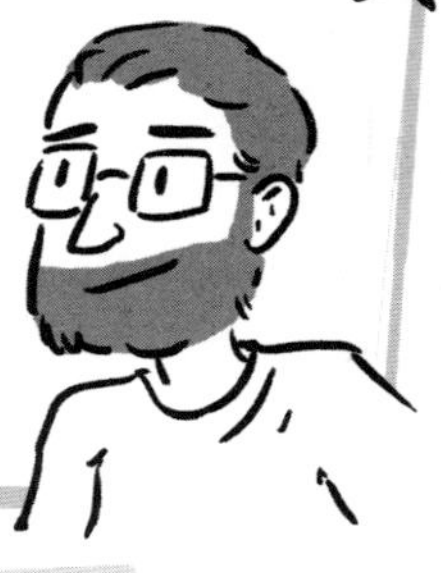

Extra resources on the web!

www.everyoneisgay.com
www.them.us
www.autostraddle.com
www.minus18.org.au
www.scarleteen.com
www.google.com